LIGUORI CATHOLIC BIBLE STUDY

Pentateuch I

CREATION AND COVENANT

WILLIAM A. ANDERSON, DMIN, PHD

Liguori
LIGUORI, MISSOURI

D0907760

Imprimi Potest:
Harry Grile, CSsR, Provincial
Denver Province, The Redemptorists

Printed with Ecclesiastical Permission and Approved for Private or Instructional Use

Nihil Obstat:
Rev. Msgr. Kevin Michael Quirk, JCD, JV
Censor Librorum

Imprimatur:
+ Michael J. Bransfield
Bishop of Wheeling-Charleston [West Virginia]
November 15, 2012

Published by Liguori Publications
Liguori, Missouri 63057

To order, call 800-325-9521
www.liguori.org

Cataloging-in-Publication Data on file with the Library of Congress

p ISBN 978-0-7648-2131-8
e ISBN 978-0-7648-2306-0

Liguori Publications, a nonprofit corporation, is an apostolate of the Redemptorists. To learn more about the Redemptorists, visit Redemptorists.com.

Printed in the United States of America
17 16 15 14 13 / 5 4 3 2 1
First Edition

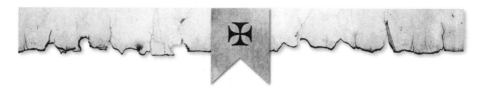

Contents

Acknowledgments 5

Introduction to *Liguori Catholic Bible Study* 7

***Lectio Divina* (Sacred Reading) 9**

How to Use This Bible-Study Companion 12
　　A Process for Sacred Reading 13
　　Group-study Formats 14

Introduction: Pentateuch I 17

Lesson 1　The Book of Genesis: Stories of Creation 21
　　Part 1: Group Study (Genesis 1—3) 22
　　Part 2: Individual Study 31

Lesson 2　From Cain to Abram 32
　　Part 1: Group Study (Genesis 4—8) 33
　　Part 2: Individual Study (Genesis 9—15) 40

Lesson 3　A Covenant With God 49
　　Part 1: Group Study (Genesis 16—18:15) 50
　　Part 2: Individual Study (Genesis 18:16—26) 55

Lesson 4　From Jacob to Joseph 66
　　Part 1: Group Study (Genesis 27—28) 67
　　Part 2: Individual Study (Genesis 29—38) 71

NOTE: The length of each Bible section varies. Group leaders should combine sections as needed to fit the number of sessions in their program.

Lesson 5   The Family of Israel Settles in Egypt 85

        Part 1: Group Study (Genesis 39—41) 86

        Part 2: Individual Study (Genesis 42—50) 90

Lesson 6   The Book of Exodus: Exodus From Egypt 100

        Part 1: Group Study (Exodus 1—3:15) 101

        Part 2: Individual Study (Exodus 3:16—7:7) 107

Lesson 7   Departure From Egypt 113

        Part 1: Group Study (Exodus 7:8—8) 114

        Part 2: Individual Study (Exodus 9—15:21) 118

Lesson 8   Ten Commandments of the Lord 128

        Part 1: Group Study (Exodus 15:22—17) 129

        Part 2: Individual Study (Exodus 18—40) 132

Acknowledgments

Bible studies and reflections depend on the help of others who read the manuscript and make suggestions. I am especially indebted to Sister Anne Francis Bartus, CSJ, DMin, whose vast experience and knowledge were very helpful in bringing this series to its final form.

This series is lovingly dedicated to the memory of my parents, Kathleen and Angor Anderson, in gratitude for all they shared with all who knew them, especially my siblings and me.

Introduction to
Liguori Catholic Bible Study

READING THE BIBLE can be daunting. It's a complex book, and many a person of goodwill has tried to read the Bible and ended up putting it down in utter confusion. It helps to have a companion, and _Liguori Catholic Bible Study_ is a solid one. Over the course of this series, you'll learn about biblical messages, themes, personalities, and events and understand how the books of the Bible rose out of the need to address new situations.

Across the centuries, people of faith have asked, "Where is God in this moment?" Millions of Catholics look to the Bible for encouragement in their journey of faith. Wisdom teaches us not to undertake Bible study alone, disconnected from the Church that was given Scripture to share and treasure. When used as a source of prayer and thoughtful reflection, the Bible comes alive.

Your choice of a Bible-study program should be dictated by what you want to get out of it. One goal of _Liguori Catholic Bible Study_ is to give readers greater familiarity with the Bible's structure, themes, personalities, and message. But that's not enough. This program will also teach you to use Scripture in your prayer. God's message is as compelling and urgent today as ever, but we get only part of the message when it's memorized and stuck in our heads. It's meant for the entire person—physical, emotional, and spiritual.

We're baptized into life with Christ, and we're called to live more fully with Christ today as we practice the values of justice, peace, forgiveness, and community. God's new covenant was written on the hearts of the people of Israel; we, their spiritual descendants, are loved that intimately by God today. _Liguori Catholic Bible Study_ will draw you closer to God, in whose image and likeness we are fashioned.

Group and Individual Study

The *Liguori Catholic Bible Study* series is intended for group and individual study and prayer. This series gives you the tools to start a study group. Gathering two or three people in a home or announcing the meeting of a Bible-study group in a parish or community can bring surprising results. Each lesson in this series contains a section to help groups study, reflect, pray, and share biblical reflections. Each lesson also has a second section for individual study.

Many people who want to learn more about the Bible don't know where to begin. This series gives them a place to start and helps them continue until they're familiar with all the books of the Bible.

Bible study can be a lifelong project, always enriching those who wish to be faithful to God's Word. When people complete a study of the whole Bible, they can begin again, making new discoveries with each new adventure into the Word of God.

Lectio Divina
(Sacred Reading)

BIBLE STUDY isn't just a matter of gaining intellectual knowledge of the Bible; it's also about gaining a greater understanding of God's love and concern for creation. The purpose of reading and knowing the Bible is to enrich our relationship with God. God loves us and gave us the Bible to illustrate that love. As Pope Benedict XVI reminds us, a study of the Bible is not only an intellectual pursuit but also a spiritual adventure that should influence our dealings with God and neighbor.

The Meaning of *Lectio Divina*

Lectio divina is a Latin expression that means "divine or sacred reading." The process for *lectio divina* consists of Scripture readings, reflection, and prayer. Many clergy, religious, and laity use *lectio divina* in their daily spiritual reading to develop a closer and more loving relationship with God. Learning about Scripture has as its purpose the living of its message, which demands a period of reflection on the Scripture passages.

Prayer and *Lectio Divina*

Prayer is a necessary element for the practice of *lectio divina*. The entire process of reading and reflecting is a prayer. It's not merely an intellectual pursuit; it's also a spiritual one. Page 16 includes an Opening Prayer for gathering one's thoughts before moving on to the passages in each section. This prayer may be used privately or in a group. For those who use the book for daily spiritual reading, the prayer for each section may be repeated each day. Some may wish to keep a journal of each day's meditation.

Pondering the Word of God

Lectio divina is the ancient Christian spiritual practice of reading the holy Scriptures with intentionality and devotion. This practice helps Christians center themselves and descend to the level of the heart to enter an inner quiet space, finding God.

This sacred reading is distinct from reading for knowledge or information, and it's more than the pious practice of spiritual reading. It is the practice of opening ourselves to the action and inspiration of the Holy Spirit. As we intentionally focus on and become present to the inner meaning of the Scripture passage, the Holy Spirit enlightens our minds and hearts. We come to the text willing to be influenced by a deeper meaning that lies within the words and thoughts we ponder.

In this space, we open ourselves to be challenged and changed by the inner meaning we experience. We approach the text in a spirit of faith and obedience as a disciple ready to be taught by the Holy Spirit. As we savor the sacred text, we let go of our usual control of how we expect God to act in our lives and surrender our hearts and consciences to the flow of the divine (*divina*) through the reading (*lectio*).

The fundamental principle of *lectio divina* leads us to understand the profound mystery of the Incarnation, "The Word became flesh," not only in history but also within us.

Praying *Lectio* Today

Before you begin, relax your body and maintain a posture of prayer (back straight, eyes shut, feet flat on the floor). Then practice these four simple actions:

1. Read a passage from Scripture or the daily Mass readings. This is known as *lectio*. (If the Word of God is read aloud, the hearers listen attentively.)

2. Pray the selected passage with attention as you listen for a specific meaning that comes to mind. Once again, the reading is listened to or silently read and reflected or meditated on. This is known as *meditatio*.

3. The exercise becomes active. Pick a word, sentence, or idea that surfaces from your consideration of the chosen text. Does the reading remind you of a person, place, or experience? If so, pray about it. Compose your thoughts and reflection into a simple word or phrase. This prayer-thought will help you remove distractions during the *lectio*. This exercise is called *oratio*.

4. In silence, with your eyes closed, quiet yourself and become conscious of your breathing. Let your thoughts, feelings, and concerns fade as you consider the selected passage in the previous step (*oratio*). If you're distracted, use your prayer word to help you return to silence. This is *contemplatio*.

This exercise can take as long as you want, but in the context of this Bible study, 10 to 20 minutes should be sufficient.

Many teachers of prayer call contemplation the prayer of resting in God, a prelude to losing oneself in the presence of God. Scripture is transformed in our hearing as we pray and allow our hearts to unite intimately with the Lord. The Word truly takes on flesh, and this time it is manifested in our flesh.

How to Use This Bible-Study Companion

THE BIBLE, along with the commentaries and reflections found in this study, will help participants become familiar with the Scripture texts and lead them to reflect more deeply on the texts' message. At the end of this study, participants will have a firm grasp of Genesis and Exodus and realize how each book offers spiritual nourishment. This study is not only an intellectual adventure, it's also a spiritual one. The reflections lead participants into their own journey with the Scripture readings.

Context

When the authors wrote the Pentateuch, they didn't simply link random stories together. They placed them in a context to stress a message. To help readers learn about each passage in relation to those around it, each lesson begins with an overview that puts the Scripture passages into context.

Part 1: Group Study

To give participants a comprehensive study of Genesis and Exodus, this book is divided into eight lessons. Lesson 1 is group study only; Lessons 2 through 8 are divided into Part 1, group study, and Part 2, individual study. For example, Lesson 2 covers passages from Genesis 4 through 15. The study group reads and discusses only Genesis 4 through 8 (Part 1). Participants privately read and reflect on Genesis 9 through 15 (Part 2).

Group study may or may not include *lectio divina*. With *lectio divina*, the group meets for ninety minutes using the format at the top of page 14. Without *lectio divina*, the group meets for one hour using the format at the bottom of page 14, and participants are urged to privately read the *lectio divina* section at the end of Part 1. It contains additional reflections on the Scripture passages studied during the group session that will take participants even further into the passages.

Part 2: Individual Study

The gospel passages not covered in Part 1 are divided into three to six shorter components, one to be studied each day. Participants who don't belong to a study group can use the lessons for private sacred reading. They may choose to reflect on one Scripture passage per day, making it possible for a clearer understanding of the Scripture passages used in their *lectio divina* (sacred reading).

A PROCESS FOR SACRED READING

Liguori Publications has designed this study to be user friendly and manageable. However, group dynamics and leaders vary. We're not trying to keep the Holy Spirit from working in your midst, thus we suggest you decide beforehand which format works best for your group. If you have limited time, you could study the Bible as a group and save prayer and reflection for personal time.

However, if your group wishes to digest and feast on sacred Scripture through both prayer and study, we recommend you spend closer to ninety minutes each week by gathering to study and pray with Scripture. *Lectio divina* (see page 9) is an ancient contemplative prayer form that moves readers from the head to the heart in meeting the Lord. We strongly suggest using this prayer form whether in individual or group study.

GROUP-STUDY FORMATS

1. Bible Study With *Lectio Divina*

About ninety minutes of group study

- ✠ Gathering and opening prayer (3–5 minutes)
- ✠ Scripture passage read aloud (5 minutes)
- ✠ Silently review the commentary and prepare to discuss it with the group (3–5 minutes)
- ✠ Discuss the Scripture passage along with the commentary and reflection (30 minutes)
- ✠ Scripture passage read aloud a second time, followed by quiet time for meditation and contemplation (5 minutes)
- ✠ Spend some time in prayer with the selected passage. Group participants will slowly read the Scripture passage a third time in silence, listening for the voice of God as they read (10–20 minutes)
- ✠ Shared reflection (10–15 minutes)
- ✠ Closing prayer (3–5 minutes)

To become acquainted with lectio divina, *see page 9.*

2. Bible Study

About one hour of group study

- ✠ Gathering and opening prayer (3–5 minutes)
- ✠ Scripture passage read aloud (5 minutes)
- ✠ Silently review the commentary and prepare to discuss it with the group (3–5 minutes)
- ✠ Discuss the Scripture passage along with the commentary and reflection (40 minutes)
- ✠ Closing prayer (3–5 minutes)

Notes to the Leader

- Bring a copy of the *New American Bible*, revised edition.
- Plan which sections will be covered each week of your Bible study.
- Read the material in advance of each session.
- Establish written ground rules. (Example: We won't keep you longer than ninety minutes; don't dominate the sharing by arguing or debating.)
- Meet in an appropriate and welcoming gathering space (church building, meeting room, house).
- Provide name tags and perhaps use a brief icebreaker for the first meeting; ask participants to introduce themselves.
- Mark the Scripture passage(s) that will be read during the session.
- Decide how you would like the Scripture to be read aloud (whether by one or multiple readers).
- Use a clock or watch.
- Provide extra Bibles (or copies of the Scripture passages) for participants who don't bring their Bible.
- Ask participants to read "Introduction: Pentateuch I" (page 17) before the first session.
- Tell participants which passages to study and urge them to read the passages and commentaries before the meeting.
- If you opt to use the *lectio divina* format, familiarize yourself with this prayer form ahead of time.

Notes to Participants

- Bring a copy of the *New American Bible*, revised edition.
- Read "Introduction: Pentateuch I" (page 17) before the first class.
- Read the Scripture passages and commentaries before each session.
- Be prepared to share and listen respectfully. (This is not a time to debate beliefs or argue.)

Opening Prayer

Leader: O God, come to my assistance,

Response: O Lord, make haste to help me.

Leader: Glory be to the Father, and to the Son, and to the Holy Spirit...

Response: ...as it was in the beginning, is now, and ever shall be, world without end. Amen.

Leader: Christ is the vine and we are the branches. As branches linked to Jesus, the vine, we are called to recognize that the Scriptures are always being fulfilled in our lives. It is the living Word of God living on in us. Come, Holy Spirit, fill the hearts of your faithful, and kindle in us the fire of your divine wisdom, knowledge, and love.

Response: Open our minds and hearts as we study your great love for us as shown in the Bible.

Reader: (Open your Bible to the assigned Scripture(s) and read in a paced, deliberate manner. Pause for one minute, listening for a word, phrase, or image that you may use in your *lectio divina* practice.)

Closing Prayer

Leader: Let us pray as Jesus taught us.

Response: Our Father...

Leader: Lord, inspire us with your Spirit as we study your Word in the Bible. Be with us this day and every day as we strive to know you and serve you and to love as you love. We believe that through your goodness and love, the Spirit of the Lord is truly upon us. Allow the words of the Bible, your Word, to capture us and inspire us to live as you live and to love as you love.

Response: Amen.

Leader: May the divine assistance remain with us always.

Response: In the name of the Father, and of the Son, and of the Holy Spirit. Amen.

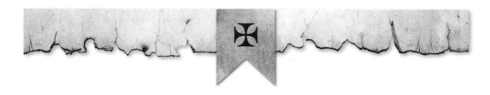

Pentateuch I

Read this overview before the first class.

The term "Pentateuch" is a Greek term that refers to the first <u>five</u> books of the Jewish and Christian Bible. Jewish tradition calls the first five books of the Bible the "Torah," meaning an Instruction or Law. This designation stems from the central theme found in these books: namely, the covenant God made with Moses on Mount Sinai and the legislation that God revealed to Moses.

Who Wrote the Pentateuch?

Until the seventeenth century, most Catholic and Jewish scholars believed that Moses wrote the entire Pentateuch, and there are still a few scholars today who hold this theory. However, in the nineteenth century, a more in-depth study of the style and content of the original writings led scholars to conclude that the books of the Pentateuch were written and edited by more than one author and that the writings of the different books and parts of the books were written at different periods of history, under different circumstances.

German scholars were able to identify these differences and could infer an approximate era when the different authors and editors took part in bringing the Pentateuch to its final form. Although we will refer to the authors of the various traditions found in the following summary as a single author, we must remember that each tradition may consist of several authors. The following is a summary of some conclusions drawn from this in-depth study of the Pentateuch:

1. J (Yahwist tradition). Around the middle of the tenth century before Christ, an author wrote about God's creation and God's dealing with the early families shortly after the creation of the world. This first author of passages found in the Pentateuch wrote about ten centuries after Abraham. German Scripture scholars from the nineteenth century after Christ noted that an author who wrote portions of the Pentateuch used a personal name for God: Yahweh. In German, the term Yahweh became Jahweh. Since the first letter of the term Jahweh was a "J" in German, the German scholars referred to the author who used this term for God as "J."

The Yahwist author (J) covers the period from the creation of the world to the journey of the Israelites in the desert. Besides using the term Yahweh for God, the Yahwist author had characteristics not found in the other writers. In the Yahwist tradition, we discover an anthropomorphic image of God. God has human qualities as shown in the Book of Genesis when Adam and Eve "heard the sound of the Lord God walking about in the Garden at the breezy time of the day" (3:8). In the biblical text, the Yahwist author pictures God as visiting Abraham and conversing with him (see Genesis 18).

The Yahwist author wrote from Judea at a time when the tribes of Israel were united in the one kingdom of Israel. Hence, the style of the writing found in the Yahwist saga is more colorful than that found in the other writers of the Pentateuch. Yahwist tradition gathers together the stories, poems, oracles, and other forms of oral messages and shapes them into an intriguing story. And when the author speaks of the mountain where Moses concludes the covenant made with God, he names the mountain Mount Sinai.

2. E (Elohist tradition). In the ninth century BC, another author wrote a narrative that later became part of the Pentateuch. It is referred to as the Elohist tradition because the author uses the more formal term of Elohim for God. His writings are designated by the letter "E." The author's style in the Elohist tradition is less colorful than those found written by the Yahwist author. Still, the fascinating story of Abraham's test when asked to sacrifice Isaac comes from the Elohist author (see Genesis 22:1–19).

The Elohist author avoids the human images of God as found in the

Yahwist writings and makes use of dreams, heavenly messengers, or majestic theophanies (visitations from God) to communicate with humans.

Toward the end of the tenth century before Christ, after the reign of King Solomon, Israel broke into two separate kingdoms, one in the north, known as Israel, and the other in the south, known as Judah. The Elohist author writes from the northern kingdom. This difference in location between the Yahwist and Elohist authors may explain why some stories are repeated with small variations. Both writers received some of the same oral stories and incorporated them into their manuscripts, but the Elohist author refers to Mount Sinai as Mount Horeb.

3. P (Priestly tradition). A later author or editor wrote about Priestly concerns, laws, and rituals that eventually found their way into the Pentateuch. This author (or authors) wrote circa 550 to 450 BC, the period of time immediately following the Israelites' return from exile in Babylon. The Priestly account, designated by the letter "P," contains a number of genealogies and presents its message in the most precise and factual manner of all other passages in the Pentateuch. Here, however, the author does show signs of poetic genius in the first story of creation, containing therein an obvious poetic balance. The Priestly author or editor not only added new material to the story, but also mingled some of the stories of both the Yahwist and Elohist authors, making it difficult at times to distinguish one source from the other.

4. D (Deuteronomist). The Deuteronomist author, referred to as "D," wrote circa the years 650 to 620 BC. The author speaks of reforms in the last Book of the Pentateuch, and these writings appear mainly in the Book of Deuteronomy.

An Important Note About Genealogies and Laws

Many people who attempt to study the Bible read as far as the lists of genealogies or laws and soon find themselves bogged down in these lists of names that mean little to them. The same is also true of the laws initially intended to instruct the daily life of the Jewish community in Israel. For many readers, attempting to navigate these genealogies and laws can become a tedious and boring struggle at times. At this point, many abandon the reading of the Bible. It is for this reason that this study suggests that the reader scan or skip the genealogies in the Bible and read the commentaries in this text. Therefore, for the purpose of this study, a brief commentary indicates to the reader that he or she can skip or scan the biblical text in these sections of Genesis and Exodus according to need. The reader will find these sections grey-scaled in this study, but if possible, participants might read the text all the same.

Genealogies: In the Pentateuch, the Priestly editor will often interrupt the story to introduce genealogies, which he uses to bind the story together. Although the genealogies help the reader in understanding the family line of the major figures found in the Pentateuch, they can also distract the reader from the flow of the story. Some names in the genealogies mean nothing to the reader and others have a significant and often subtle message. In most cases, the genealogies were not part of the original narrative.

Laws and Rituals: Many people who read or study the Bible find its story extremely interesting until chapter 20 in Exodus, after Moses receives the Ten Commandments. The laws that follow in chapters 21, 22, and 23 are later additions to the commandments, some of which address issues for people who are no longer nomads, but who have settled down in the Promised Land. The Priestly author who wrote around the sixth or fifth century before Christ inserts many laws and rituals in the text as though they were given to Moses, an event that seems highly unlikely. The present text will give a short commentary on the laws but will not add a reflection. The reader may decide to scan the laws or skip over them and move on to the narrative sections of the Bible.

Note that many of the reflections in the *lectio divina* link the Pentateuch stories with segments from the New Testament. Using this approach enables the reader to understand more fully the relationship of the Old Testament to the New Testament. Jesus said that he did not come to abolish the law or the prophets, but to fulfill them (see Matthew 5:17).

LESSON 1

The Book of Genesis
Stories of Creation
GENESIS 1–3

"That is why a man leaves his father and mother and clings to his wife, and the two of them become one body" (2:24).

Opening Prayer (SEE PAGE 16)

Context

In the Book of Genesis, we encounter two stories that describe the creation of the world and God's special creation of human beings. In the first story of creation, God creates the world in seven days and declares that all of creation is good. This story moves its audience from the creation of light to the peak of creation, that is, the creation of human beings in the image and likeness of God.

It is in the second story of creation that God creates a man out of the dust of the earth. Likewise, God creates animals as a companion for the man but recognizes the need for human beings to relate to other human beings. So God creates woman by taking a rib from the man, showing that women and men are equal to each other. The unity and equality are expressed as the man exclaims, "This one, at last, is bone of my bones and flesh of my flesh" (2:23).

PART 1: GROUP STUDY (GENESIS 1—3)

Read aloud Genesis 1—3.

1:1-13 The First Three Days of Creation

The account in the first story of creation comes from the Priestly author (P) who wrote somewhere around the fifth century before Christ. Although the Priestly author was the last editor of the Book of Genesis, the Priestly story of creation appears first, since the historical books are presented in the Bible in a chronological order and not in the order in which they were written. Both stories of creation in the Bible do not present exact history, although they do convey basic theological truths about creation. It is essential to understand that it is the theological message in the biblical text that is inspired, not the scientific or historical.

The Priestly story of creation begins with an image of an earth without form or shape, with darkness covering a deep abyss and a strong wind sweeping over the waters. When God creates, all is dark, foreboding, and chaotic. The story does not tell us that God created the world out of nothing, since this chaotic world exists, but out of this chaos God creates the heavens and the earth. This is the beginning of creation, a time when the earth was without form or shape. Although the author makes no mention of God's pre-existence, a psalmist expresses the belief of the people when he writes, "Before the mountains were born, the earth and the world brought forth, from eternity to eternity you are God" (Psalm 90:2). The author of the first story of creation presumes the pre-existence of God without referring to it.

God begins to put order into this watery chaos by first creating light and separating it from darkness. In doing this, God is creating an orderly sequence of day and night. In ancient times, many people did not connect light with the sun but saw light as something unique in itself. God calls the light "day" and the darkness "night," an action which not only shows that God created light and darkness, but that God names them as day and night. When the author says that evening came and morning followed, he writes using the Semitic practice that speaks of a new day in this way, that is from sundown to sundown—one day to the next. The refrain, "Evening came, and morning followed," will be repeated for each new day.

When God creates light, God saw that it was good. Likewise, the refrain that God saw each act of creation as good will be repeated throughout the creation story. This refrain, along with the refrain about evening and morning, is the underlying poetic format of the creation story.

The reader of the creation events should keep in mind that this is a story told to teach an inspired message, that God is the creator of an ordered universe and all that is in the universe is good. Whether one day was twenty-four hours or a hundred years is irrelevant to the author, since he was not addressing that issue. To attempt to explain the age of the world by reading this story in a literal, scientific, and historical sense is futile, since this was not the author's intent while penning this text.

On the second day, God separates the water above the earth from the water below the earth. The author seems to say that God speaks ("Let there be a dome") and the dome came into being, but then he says that God made the dome. Although both ideas could coincide, the differences could point to the editor receiving two separate renditions of the creation story and preserving them both in his account. These differences will be found as the story of creation continues. The dome seems to be some type of huge, translucent metal holding the upper ocean away from the lower water. God gives a name to the sky. The people of ancient times looked up and saw blue, the color of water, and they experienced rain as coming from the heavens, as though someone were opening floodgates in the dome and allowing the rain to come down. In the story of Noah and the Flood, we read that "the floodgates of the sky opened" (7:11).

On the third day, God's word gathers the water under the sky into basins, thus allowing the dry land to appear. God named the dry land "earth," and the basin of water as "sea." The refrain, "God saw it was good," appears again in the text. On this day, there is a double creation when God's Word has the earth bring forth vegetation. Note that God does not directly create the vegetation but has the earth bring it forth. And God saw that it was good.

1:14—2:4a The Last Four Days of Creation

The Priestly author of the first story of creation continues to exhibit a poetic format as he balances the last three days of creation with the first three. What God has separated on the first three days of creation, God now populates on the last three days. The first day is parallel to the fourth, the second to the fifth, and the third to the sixth.

On the fourth day, God provides lights in the dome for people to identify the feasts, the days, and the years. Although God has created light from darkness on the first day, God now creates lights in the dome of the sky on the fourth day, the parallel day. The editor, who previously told us that God's word spoke the lights in the dome into existence, now states that God makes them, designating the greater light (sun) to govern the day, and the lesser one (the moon) to govern the nights. The stars are simply mentioned without conferring any governing powers to them. The greater light and the lesser one have the specific duty of governing the day and night, all in an orderly fashion. God saw that it was good, and evening came and morning followed.

On the fifth day, God populates the sky that God created on the second day. The waters teem with living creatures, sea monsters, crawling living creatures, and birds fly in the space beneath the dome. God saw it was good and blessed the creatures so that they would be fertile and multiply. Evening came and morning followed.

On the sixth day, God calls upon the earth to bring forth every living creature and animals, wild and tame. On the third day, when God separated land from water, God had the land bring forth vegetation. On this sixth day, the parallel day, God calls upon the earth to bring forth animals and crawling creatures. God saw that it was good. On the sixth day, God creates human beings, but in a different manner. Humans do not come from the earth, but from God. God uses the plural form when God says, "Let us make human beings in our image, after our likeness" (1:26), as though God is speaking with someone. Some later commentators view the use of the plural as a hidden reference to the Trinity, while others recall that in the ancient Near East, people imagined God as presiding over a heavenly court of some type. The image and likeness of God used in this passage refer to a spiritual, not a physical, likeness to God.

This image and likeness of God lifts human beings above the animals, so God blesses them and makes them male and female, fertile human beings so that they may multiply, fill the earth, and subdue it. Procreation and sexuality are God's idea, given for the good of humanity. The call to multiply is a gift and a command from God. Since human beings are made in the image and likeness of God, they have dominion over vegetation as well as living and crawling creatures. The author crowns God's words in creation with the final statement, "And so it happened," and when God looked on all that was made, God found it very good. Evening came and morning followed.

In this first creation story, the Priestly author moved from the lesser to the greater, professing that human beings are the peak of God's creation. Light and darkness, sky and water, land and vegetation, sun and moon, sea creatures and birds, animals, and crawling creatures, all are given to human beings, the peak of creation, to subdue and use properly. God gives human beings every seed-bearing plant and seed-bearing fruit for food. According to the Priestly author, human beings and animals were initially intended to live on plants and fruit, but God will later change that plan when God makes a covenant with Noah after the Flood (9:3).

On the seventh day, when God's work of creation was completed, God rested. Although the Priestly author makes no mention of the observance of the Sabbath rest for others, he does say that God rested on the seventh day and made it holy.

2:4b–25 The Second Story of Creation

When the Old Testament was edited, or pieced together, the editor found two stories of creation. Rather than make them consistent with each other, the Priestly editor simply placed one story after the other and joins them together with the sentence: "This is the story of the heavens and the earth at their creation" (2:4a). The story from the Yahwist author (J) begins right after this opening sentence. The author of the second story of creation wrote the story far in advance of the first story of creation, but it appears second in the Bible, which is appropriate due to its style and its totality that continues for several chapters.

The first Priestly story of creation is more measured and methodical, listing one day after the other, while the second story comes from a brilliant storyteller who weaves together a magnificent story of a concerned and involved God, who rewards, punishes, and remains a constant companion. When the Lord made the earth and the heavens, the world was a barren waste with no shrubs or grass, because the Lord God had sent no rain to nourish the earth. Since the world view at the time this account was written imaged the earth sitting somehow above water, the author speaks of a single stream welling up out of the earth (the underworld) and watering the ground. This seems to be God's Garden, the only place where water enriches the thirsty ground. The author tells us that until the creation of the first human being, there was no one to cultivate the land.

God takes the dust of the land and forms a human being out of it. In the original Hebrew, there is a play on words in the biblical text. The Hebrew word for a "human being" was adam and the Hebrew word for ground was adama. Molding a human being out of dust is not enough. God breathes into the nostrils of the human being, a sign of the divine breath being given to a person. Although the story shows the connection between a human being and the land, it does not point to a separation between the body made from the dust and the spirit of God. The idea of a separate body and soul is a result of Greek thinking, a thought process not inherent to the Israelites. When the breath of God comes into this first human, he becomes a living being.

God plants a Garden in Eden in the east and places the human being there. The Garden is like a park, a paradise, where the man will reside and care for and till the Garden. Some would see the Garden as a place for God to enjoy rather than humans, since the work of humans is to till and care for it. The Garden paradise included trees that were beautiful and produced excellent food. And in the middle of the Garden stood the tree of life and the tree of knowledge of good and evil. We will later learn that the tree of knowledge of good and evil provides knowledge for Adam and Eve that comes from experience and personal involvement. The naming of these two trees could derive from two oral traditions which are joined together in this story.

Interrupting the flow of the narrative is a supposed geographical location for Eden. The interruption in the story seems to situate the Garden outside Eden. The story indicates that there are four rivers that branch from a river originating in Eden. Two of them, the Tigris and Euphrates, are identifiable, but the position of Eden is still confusing. In ancient times, people were not as knowledgeable about the geography of the seas and rivers. The names of the rivers and the attempt to locate Eden is most likely more symbolic than real.

Although an earlier verse tells us that God placed man in the Garden (2:8), the author repeats that God settles man in the Garden to cultivate and care for it. The reading would imply that work or co-creation is given for human beings from the beginning of their existence, since God directs the man to cultivate the Garden before any sin is committed. We will later learn that the punishment for sin is not that humans must work, but that the land will become difficult to cultivate and labor will be difficult. The Lord God tells the man that he may eat of any tree in the Garden except of the tree of knowledge of good and evil. If he eats of that tree, he will die. The tree of knowledge of good and evil is in the middle of the Garden, where it will have to be passed each day.

In telling the story of God's creation, the Yahwist author realizes the need for human relationship. In the story, God, recognizing that it is not good for man to be alone and in need of a helper, creates animals and birds out of the ground and brings them to the man to name. To the Israelites, naming something or someone implies dominion over it. In allowing Adam to name the animals, God is giving him dominion over them. The man names wild and tame animals and the birds, but none of them proves to be a suitable partner.

The Lord God casts Adam into a deep sleep and takes out one of his ribs and makes the rib into a woman. When Adam sees the woman, he exclaims with joy that this one "is bone of my bones and flesh of my flesh," and he names her the generic name of "woman," since she has been taken out of man (see 2:23). He will later give her the more specific name of "Eve." Unlike the animals who are created from the ground, separate from Adam, the woman is taken from a rib of Adam, which shows equality and a need of man and woman for each other.

The second creation story, like the first, stresses that the two become one. Although the author is speaking about the first man and woman in this story, he is establishing the principle for all people, namely that a man and woman leave father and mother and the two become one body, which means the two become one in God's eyes. They were both one flesh before God took the rib from Adam, and now, in God's plan, they are both again one flesh. They are both naked, but they feel no shame. Nakedness expresses the openness they have for each other, an openness applying not only to their bodies, but also to the unity and openness of mind. With childlike simplicity, they are not conscious of any shame.

3:1–24 Expulsion from Eden

The Yahwist author continues his story by stating that the serpent was the most cunning of all the wild animals God had made. The people of ancient times saw snakes as cunning and wise, and symbols of immortality and fertility. The author here does not refer to the snake as the devil but uses a play on words in the original language by using the same word for "naked" and "cunning." The snake is cunning in its approach to the woman, acting as one who is concerned about Eve, and one who portrays God as the cunning one.

The snake asks if God forbade them from eating from any of the trees in the Garden. But the woman answers that they are not allowed to eat of the fruit in the middle of the Garden. Placement of the tree in the middle of the Garden becomes significant in intensifying the temptation, as temptation becomes central to human existence, always alluring people to taste the forbidden fruit. This warning for the first humans is not only that they cannot eat the fruit, but they cannot even touch it. If they do, they will die. When the Scriptures speak of death, they do not always refer to physical death, but spiritual death. The death Adam and Eve will experience is the death of expulsion from life in paradise, although they do not understand its meaning as yet.

The cunning snake tells the woman that she will not die, but that God knows that she and her husband will be like gods, knowing good and evil. The woman sees the tree as good for eating and even more so as alluring for gaining knowledge. She eats the fruit and shares it with her husband. As a result, they understand the evil they committed by disobeying God, and they lose the innocence of child-like simplicity, recognizing that they are naked. They sew fig leaves together to protect their nakedness and are no longer totally open, even with each other.

The Yahwist author presents God in human terms, picturing God as strolling in the Garden at the breezy time of day. God has to call out and ask the man where he is, and the man admits that he himself is separated from God because of his nakedness. The author already told us that the man and the woman sewed fig leaves together and covered their nakedness, but the real nakedness they experience was not a nakedness of body but one where they stand shamefully before God with their sin. God asks two questions, knowing the answer to each. Who told them they were naked; and have they eaten the forbidden fruit? The man blames the woman for his sin, and the woman blames the snake, so God curses the snake, who would now crawl on its belly in the dust.

There will be enmity and conflict between the woman's offspring and the snake, which in time will be interpreted as the devil. God tells the woman that she shall bear children in toil and pain, and the women shall depend on their husbands who will rule over them. The man will struggle with thorns and thistles in tilling the land that he will till. He will provide food with the sweat of his brow until the day he returns to dust. The authority of the man becomes apparent as he names his wife Eve, which means "mother of all the living." The reader must keep in mind that the story was developed in a patriarchal society where men dominated women. By naming Eve "mother of all the living," the man looks for life to continue.

God shows concern for the man and his wife by making garments of skins for them. Speaking to the heavenly court, God expresses fear that human beings may eat of the tree of life and live forever. God therefore banishes the man and woman from the Garden of Eden and stations a cherubim and a fiery revolving sword east of the Garden of Eden to guard against any entry into the Garden.

Review Questions

1. What implications for our understanding of God's creation can you derive from the first creation story? From the second?
2. Why is the tree of good and evil placed in the center of the Garden? Explain and discuss.

Closing Prayer (SEE PAGE 16)

Pray the closing prayer now or after *lectio divina*.

Lectio Divina (SEE PAGE 9)

Relax your body and maintain a posture of prayer (back straight, eyes shut, feet flat on the floor). This exercise can take as long as you want, but in the context of this Bible study, 10 to 20 minutes should be sufficient.

The meditations that follow are provided only to help group participants use this prayer form, but note that *lectio* is intended to bring one to a place of prayerful contemplation where the Word of God speaks to the hearer from his or her heart. (See page 9 for further instruction.)

The First Three Days of Creation (1:1–13)

A man and woman walked along the seashore one day and blessed God for the beauty of the vast ocean in front of them. Another couple climbed a mountain and peered out over green valleys and said, "God is good." A small eleven-year-old boy brought home a flower from a field and gave it to his mother and said, "God gave this to you." An elderly couple sitting on a porch on a warm day laughed together as they both put hands on aching backs when they stood, and proclaimed, "God has been good to us." And God looked at all the people who learned of God's love throughout creation, and God saw that creation was good.

✠ *What can I learn from this passage?*

The Last Four Days of Creation (1:14—2:4a)

On a sunny morning, a woman and her husband were fishing by the side of a stream, listening to the birds and watching a squirrel scurry from one tree to another. They were enjoying the gifts of God's creation and marveled at the silence of the morning broken only by the singing of birds and an occasional ripple in the water caused by a fish catching breakfast. Their twenty–year-old daughter was watching her three siblings, two boys and a girl, still asleep in the cabin they rented for their vacation. The couple worked hard all week, and now they were enjoying God's gift of nature. Finally, the woman smiled and said, "We have all this, and we have each other." The man smiled and said, "And God saw it was good!"

✠ *What can I learn from this passage?*

The Second Creation Story (2:4b–25)

If God were to tell us that we could go to the Garden of Eden where life was easy, the water for swimming was perfect, it rained only at night, and we had whatever food or drink we wanted, we might think this to be wonderful. But if God added that we had to go alone with no human companions, most of us would immediately refuse the offer. God created the Garden of Paradise, but real paradise consists of loving and being loved, and knowing it. As God said, "It is not good for the man (or woman) to be alone." Human beings need each other.

✠ *What can I learn from this passage?*

Expulsion from Eden (3)

The cunning snake in the story touches on our desire to control our own destiny. If we eat of the fruit, that is to give into temptation, we will be like God. Because the fruit is forbidden, it looks more mysterious, more tempting. So we take the fruit and suddenly realize how naked and vulnerable we are. We want to hide ourselves from others by not unveiling or wanting them to know our secrets. We may even want to hide ourselves from God and make excuses, blaming others for our failures. But we have the comfort of knowing that God still wants to walk with us, no matter what we've done. God never leaves us.

✠ *What can I learn from this passage?*

PART 2: INDIVIDUAL STUDY

This lesson does not have an individual-study section.

From Cain to Abram

GENESIS 4—15

When I bring clouds over the earth, and the bow appears in the clouds, I will remember my covenant between me and you and every living creature—every mortal being—so that the waters will never again become a flood to destroy every mortal being (9:14–15).

Opening Prayer (SEE PAGE 16)

Context

Part 1: Genesis 4—8 God accepts Abel's offering over that of his brother Cain, who kills Abel. God tells Cain that his brother's blood cries out to heaven from the ground and punishes him by making Cain and his descendants wanderers on the earth. Adam and Eve conceive another son named Seth. The world becomes so sinful that God chooses Noah and his family to escape from a mighty flood over the land. Noah builds an ark and brings his family and animals into the ark. The family of Noah and all the animals survive the Flood.

Part 2: Genesis 9—15 God makes a covenant with Noah and puts a rainbow in the sky as a sign of the covenant, promising never again to destroy the world with a flood. Noah's second son, Ham, sins against Noah, and Noah curses him and his descendants. Later in time, when God sees the people building a tower with its top in the sky, God confuses their languages. Abram, his wife, Sarai, and his nephew, Lot, appear in the narrative as nomads migrating over the land. In Egypt, when Pharaoh is informed that Sarai is Abram's sister, he takes her into his home, but a plague strikes him and his household. Pharaoh berates Abram for his deception. Later, Abram and Lot part so that each may shepherd their herds peacefully. In time, Abram must rescue Lot from men who capture him.

PART 1: GROUP STUDY (GENESIS 4—8)

Read aloud Genesis 4:1–16 and 6—8.

4:1–16 Cain and Abel

Adam has intercourse with his wife, and she conceives a son whom she names Cain. She later conceives another son named Abel. When both sons grow older, they bring an offering to God. Cain, a tiller of the land, brings an offering from the fruit of the land, and Abel, a tender of flocks, brings the fatty portion of the firstlings of his flock. For some unknown and unexplained reason, God looks with favor on Abel's offering and rejects Cain's. God warns Cain that sin lies at his door. The Yahwist author speaks of sin as though sin is an animal lying in wait for its prey.

Cain kills his brother Abel, committing the first murder in the Bible, and God challenges Cain, asking about Abel. Cain's curt response is, "Am I my brother's keeper?" The presumed answer that is found throughout the Scriptures is "Yes." God states that the blood of his brother Abel cries out from the ground. According to the Book of Numbers, blood was sacred as the seat of life, and the blood of unpunished murders pollutes the ground (Numbers 35:33).

God punishes Cain by telling him that the land would no longer produce for him, thus making Cain, who was once a tiller of the land, now a wanderer. Cain fears for his life as a constant wanderer, but God put some type of mark, possibly a tattoo, to protect him. The use of tattooing for tribal marks on wanderers was a common practice. Cain settles in the land of Nod, a symbolic name indicating one who wanders, not a specific location.

4:17—5 The Family Line of Adam and Eve

(Read "Note About Genealogies" in the "Introduction: Pentateuch I," page 19. You may skip or scan the biblical text in this section.)

Cain's wife conceived and bore a son named Enoch. Cain, who was not a nomad, founded a city and named it after Enoch. Four generations after Enoch are quickly mentioned. Enoch became the father of Irad, Irad the father of Mehujael, Mehujael becomes the father of Methusael, who then becomes the father of Lamech. Lamech has two wives who give him three sons who are ancestors of a developing civilization. From Lamech came Jabal, whose offspring dwell in tents and keep livestock; Jubal, whose offspring played the lyre and reed pipe; and Tubalcain, whose offspring forge instruments of bronze and iron. Because of this history beginning with Cain, Cain becomes recognized by some as the father of civilization. Civilization, with all its advantages, does not solve the split between people and God, as the story of Lamech illustrates. The sin of Cain becomes even more bitter with his offspring.

God provides a glimmer of hope as Adam and Eve give birth to Seth, whom Eve views as a replacement for Abel. Seth had a son named Enosh. At that time, people began to invoke the Lord by name. The Yahwist author places the beginning of the use of the name "Yahweh" here in the primeval era, whereas the Priestly tradition will place its first usage in a revelation of the divine name given to Moses in Exodus. God tells Moses, "I am the LORD. As God the Almighty I appeared to Abraham, Isaac, and Jacob, but by my name, Lord, I did not make myself known to them" (6:2–3).

The Priestly editor takes the descendants found in the seven generations in the Yahwist story in chapter 4 and joins them to his genealogy of ten generations in chapter 5. The genealogies in chapter 5 move from Adam to Noah's three sons. In both genealogies, the editor ends with three names which signify some type of action or development. In ancient Babylon's lists of genealogies, the ages of those on the list were exceedingly long. Since the Priestly author likely spent some time in Babylon and was influenced by the Babylonian genealogies, the ages of those in the Israelite genealogy were likewise exceptionally long. Some commentators speculate that the shorter lives of those after the Flood show the weakening of the relationship between human beings and God. It is difficult to determine that this was the intention of the authors, who most likely inflated the ages for the sake of some message, whatever it was.

Some commentators speculate that there was a book of genealogies which the Priestly editor used for the lists he presents in Genesis. Significant in the list is Enoch, whom the author describes as one who "walked with God and he was no longer here, for God took him" (5:24). From this, some speculate that Enoch, like Elijah, did not die, but that God took him. Enoch's name will appear again in later scriptural texts. Enoch fathered Methuselah, who lived to the age of 967, the longest age in the genealogy. From this came a popular expression which refers to an elderly person as being "as old as Methuselah."

In Genesis 3:17, God cursed the ground because of Adam's sin and declared that tilling it will demand great toil. When the genealogy names Noah, it adds a line from the Yahwist author which states that Noah will bring relief from the curse God placed on the ground (5:29). This could be a reference to Noah's successful planting of a vineyard (9:20). The genealogy ends by naming Noah's three sons, who continue to play a role in the Yahwist saga.

6:1–13 The Corruption of Sin

The Yahwist author draws from legends about heavenly beings, some of whom were evil and defiant and who saw how beautiful the daughters of the human beings were. Apparently these women were mighty as well as beautiful, so the heavenly beings (sons of God) took them as wives. The Hebrews referred to a group of giant heroes who existed around this time as the Nephilim, who were men of renown. The Nephilim were not the ones referred to as the "sons of God," as some later writers thought. The sons of God who marry the daughters of men produce offspring different from the Nephilim. As a result of the rebellious union between the sons of God and the daughters of human beings, God apparently punishes human beings by allowing them to live only 120 years, far shorter than the previous life span.

The story of the Flood comes from a mingling of the Yahwist and Priestly accounts which have their origins in Mesopotamian flood stories. The

Yahwist author describes God's great disappointment with human beings who are prone toward evil. The author notes that their actions disturbed God who regretted creating them. Because God sees a link between human beings and the total environment, God intends to destroy human beings, animals, crawling creatures, and birds of the air. After the Flood, God will make a covenant with the surviving human beings and all living creatures. A note of salvation appears in the narrative as the author tells us that Noah found favor with God.

6:14—7:5 Preparation for the Flood

At this point, the Priestly author takes over the narrative, reminding the reader that Noah, who walked blamelessly with God, had three sons, Shem, Ham, and Japheth. When God sees that the rest of the earth was corrupt and filled with lawlessness, God informs Noah about the impending destruction of all mortals with the earth.

God directs Noah to build an ark with an assortment of compartments and to cover it inside and out with pitch, which is a substance made from tar, still used today for waterproofing. In a Babylonian epic of Gilgamesh, which provides some aspects of Noah's story, Gilgamesh receives the order to build a similar type of houseboat and to cover it with pitch. God describes the length and width of the ark, referring to its measurements in cubits. A cubit was about eighteen inches and was measured from the forearm to the tip of the middle finger. The size of the ark in our form of measuring would be about 440 by 73 by 44 feet. It is to have three floors (as found in the Gilgamesh epic), with an opening for daylight about a cubit below the roof and a side door.

In the midst of predicting the devastation of the flood, God promises to make a covenant with Noah. Noah, his wife, his sons and their wives are to go into the ark. The Priestly author who is writing this section has God direct Noah to bring two of every animal, bird, and crawling creature, male as well as female. The author makes no mention of clean or unclean animals but seeks to provide for the continuation of all living creatures. On a practical note, God states that they are to bring food and to store it as provisions for all. The Priestly author, who sees all as taking place according to God's command, notes that Noah did as God directed. Since divine speech is important as we saw in the first creation story, God speaks to Noah seven times in the Flood story.

The story of the Flood as presented by the Yahwist author and the Priestly author now becomes more closely entwined. Since Noah is the only one found righteous by God, God tells Noah and his household to enter the ark. The hand of the Yahwist author is seen clearly here as God directs Noah to take seven pairs of clean animals and one pair of unclean animals, male and female, into the ark. He is also to take seven pairs of birds to assure that their species continues to exist. The reason for taking seven pairs of clean animals is that some of them will be used for sacrifice. Since the unclean animals will not be sacrificed, one pair of each would suffice to continue the species. God decreed that in seven days rain will fall on the earth for forty days and forty nights.

7:6—8 The Great Flood

For a second time, the author repeats that Noah and his family went into the ark. This second entry into the ark illustrates that two separate sources are being used here. All the animals, clean and unclean, enter the ark as God commanded. When Noah was 600 years old, the waters of the Flood came upon the earth. The Flood follows the Priestly image of the world as found on the second day of creation, as the water wells up from below and the floodgates of heaven open up. For forty days the rains came.

Evidence of the Priestly author continues to show as the Lord shuts Noah, his family, every kind of animal, crawling creature, and bird into the ark. Since the Priestly author believes that the distinction between clean and unclean animals and sacrifice does not take place until God gives the Law to Moses on Sinai, the author allows for pairs of all types of living creatures to come into the ark. The Flood continued for forty days, and the ark floated to fifteen cubits above the highest mountain—just enough room for the ark to float above them. And every living thing on earth was destroyed.

After 150 days, a new creation began as God made a wind sweep over the waters in a manner similar to God breathing over the waters in the first story of creation. The fountains of the abyss and the floodgates of the sky were closed, as happened on the second day of the first story of creation. Noah released a raven that flew over the waters until they subsided. Afterward, he released a dove that returned after finding no place to land. He waited a week and sent out that same dove who came back with an olive branch, which indicated that the water was subsiding. A week later, he sent out a dove that did not return.

When Noah, his family, and all living creatures left the ark, a new creation was begun. They were to travel over the earth, be fertile, and multiply. Noah, who brought with him the ritually clean animals for sacrifice, built an altar and offered burnt sacrifices to the Lord. In the Gilgamesh epic, the gods smelled the sweet odor of Gilgamesh's burnt offering and they repented of destroying the human race. In the same way, the author pictures God as smelling the sweet odor of Noah's burnt offering and promising never again to curse the ground because of human beings. So God pledges never again to obliterate living beings with a flood. According to the text, all days, all seasons, and day and night shall never cease; and the seasons will continue as before.

Review Questions

1. What answer would God give to Cain's question, "Am I my brother's keeper?"
2. Why did God choose only Noah and his family?
3. What comparisons do you see between the two creation stories and the story of the Flood?

Closing Prayer (SEE PAGE 16)

Pray the closing prayer now or after *lectio divina*.

Lectio Divina (SEE PAGE 9)

Relax your body and maintain a posture of prayer (back straight, eyes shut, feet flat on the floor). This exercise can take as long as you want, but in the context of this Bible study, 10 to 20 minutes should be sufficient.

The meditations that follow are provided only to help group participants use this prayer form, but note that *lectio* is intended to bring one to a place of prayerful contemplation where the Word of God speaks to the hearer from his or her heart. (See page 9 for further instruction.)

Cain and Abel (4:1–16)

Jesus teaches that we are all neighbors (brothers and sisters to each other), and tells a story of a good Samaritan who lives up to his call as a neighbor by having concern for a stranger in a ditch. He washes his wounds and takes him to an inn, telling the innkeeper that he will pay the stranger's bill in full on his return (see Luke 10:25–37). The first two neighbors who ignored the man in the ditch did not see themselves as neighbors to the man. They were not their brother's or sister's keeper. In God's creation, we are all brothers and sisters in Christ, and we are meant to have a loving concern for one another.

✠ *What can I learn from this passage?*

The Corruption of Sin (6:1–13)

The serpent in this story tempts Adam and Eve by enticing them to eat the forbidden fruit, suggesting that they will be like God. Strangely, sin makes us less like God. We are called to love as God loves and to use our life for the sake of God and others. The problem that happens when evil is rampant is that people forget that all life belongs to God. There were many good people in the world when Jesus came, but none of them had the power to overcome evil. We needed that one good person to save us. Jesus' ark was not a boat, but a cross. In Jesus, a new creation is begun just as a new creation began when Noah saved his family and the animals in the ark.

✠ *What can I learn from this passage?*

The Great Flood (7:6—8)

A child and an adult come to the font for baptism. The presider welcomes them in the name of the community and a few moments later blesses the baptismal water. Then, the presider recalls the waters of the great Flood which brought about a new creation. Now, in the waters of baptism, a new creation is about to begin. Paul the Apostle says that in baptism, we die in Christ and are raised to a new life in him. Each of us who celebrates the sacrament of baptism has the call to make this new creation in Christ a living reality by loving God and our neighbor as ourselves. The waters lead us to a new creation.

✠ *What can I learn from this passage?*

PART 2: INDIVIDUAL STUDY (GENESIS 9—15)

Day 1: Covenant With Noah (9)

In the first story of creation, God tells human beings to be fertile, multiply, and fill the earth. Now, in this renewed creation, God gives the same directive to Noah and his sons. God gives humans dominion over the animals in both creation stories, but God speaks here of the fear and dread of human beings experienced by the animals, birds, crawling creatures, and fish of the sea. God places them all in the control of humans.

Because of the human propensity to violence, God permits humans to consume meat, whereas before they were to eat only vegetation. Since the ancients regard blood to be sacred, the Israelites were banned from consuming meat with blood in it. Because Noah, who is now the new father of humanity, received this law about not eating meat with blood in it from God before God established specific rules for Jews at the time of Moses, they saw this law as binding on all people.

In the Acts of the Apostles, when the Jewish Christian leaders exempt the Gentile Christians from some of the regulations of the Mosaic Law, they explicitly mention that the Gentiles must still follow the rule of not eating meat of animals with the lifeblood still in it (15:20, 29). Because human beings have the dignity of being made in the image and likeness of God, God will demand an accounting of any animal or human who kills a human being. This accounting could demand that some human being kill that animal or person.

God establishes a covenant with Noah and all his descendants and with every living creature that was with Noah in the ark. The covenant assures that God will never again destroy the earth by waters. As a sign of the covenant between Noah and every living creature for all ages to come, God sets a bow in the clouds. The bow will serve as a reminder of the covenant to humans and to God. The bow, which is sometimes seen as a rainbow during or after rainstorms, represents a weapon used in hunting with a bow and arrow. God's bow is large and beautiful. The author makes use of a literary device known as doublets to reinforce his message. He speaks of establishing a covenant in verses 9, 11, 12, and 17, and of God laying down God's bow in verses 14 and 16.

The author names Noah as a man of the soil who was the first to plant a vineyard. Noah, after drinking some of the wine from the vineyard, becomes intoxicated and was lying naked in his tent when his son Ham saw him. When Ham tells his brothers about his father's nakedness, apparently in the form of ridicule, the brothers take a robe and, holding it on their shoulders, walk backward into the tent and cover Noah's nakedness without looking at him. When Noah awakens and learns from Ham's brothers what has happened, he curses Ham's offspring, Canaan, predicting that Ham's offspring would be the lowest of slaves to his brothers. Noah rewards Shem and Japheth with a blessing, making Canaan a slave to the offspring of the brothers.

In the Ancient Near East, the son had the duty of protecting the honor of his father when his father was drunk. Ham dishonors his father with a twofold sin, first by looking on his father's nakedness, and second by telling his brothers about it. Although it may seem wrong that Noah curses Ham's son, Canaan, the story apparently looks to later events in the life of Israel, when the Israelites were in habitual clashes with the Canaanites. The other two brothers are blessed since they refused to dishonor their father and covered his nakedness without looking upon him in his disgrace.

Lectio Divina

Spend 8 to 10 minutes in silent contemplation of the following passage:

In ancient times, honoring one's father and mother was the most important after one's relationship with God. When Noah's son, Ham, dishonored him, Noah cursed his son. From the story, we learn a lesson for our world today. When we teach children to honor their parents, we must also remind adult children of the need to honor and care for their elderly parents, no matter what their condition. After the first three commandments that treat one's relationship with God comes the next most important command, namely to honor our parents. This command is that important.

✠ *What can I learn from this passage?*

The Table of Nations (10)

(Read "Note About Genealogies" in the "Introduction: Pentateuch I," page 19. You may skip or scan the biblical text in this section.)

Noah received the command to be fertile and multiply and fill all the earth. The table of nations, as this section is sometimes called, tells of the offspring of Shem, Ham, and Japheth and how their families multiplied and filled the earth. The family of Japheth had their center in Asia Minor (present-day Turkey). The family of Ham lived in a vast area in and around Egypt. Shem is the father of the Semitic peoples, which includes Israel. He is the father of Eber, whose name may be related to the name "Hebrew." If this is true, then this postulates a wider group of Eber (Hebrews) of which the Israelites were a part.

Day 2: The Tower of Babel (11:1–9)

When human beings were evicted from the Garden of Eden, they departed east from the Garden (see 3:14). Chapter 11 begins as though all the events from being expelled out of the Garden to the present did not take place, since the people are not migrating toward the east, but from the east. This story about building the Tower of Babel stands alone. In contrast to the Lord's command to be fertile, multiply, and fill the earth, the people who all speak the same language decide not to fill the earth but to build a city and a tower and then remain there. The human image of the Lord as found in the writings of the Yahwist author continues as the Lord comes down, like a human being, to see the city. The Lord worries that the people will be able to do whatever they wish unless the Lord confuses their language so that they will not be able to understand each other. The author is pointing to sin as a reason for different languages.

The temptation of humans wanting to be like gods continues, a theme also presented in the second creation story. As a result of not understanding each other, the people do not finish the tower and scatter all over the earth. The name Babel means the "gate of god" to the Babylonians, but the Hebrew word "Babal" means "the confused." In our current-day idiom, when we do not understand someone who is speaking, we may sometimes use the expression, "What are you babbling about?"

Lectio Divina

Spend 8 to 10 minutes in silent contemplation of the following passage:

Jesus' message touches every part of the world today, and people who speak different languages share a common belief in Jesus. Just as disunity came as a result of the building of the Tower of Babel, unity comes through the gift of the Holy Spirit given to people of faith throughout the world. With Christ, we are not alienated from each other but are spiritually joined as one.

✠ *What can I learn from this passage?*

Descendants From Shem to Abram (11:10–32)

(Read "Note About Genealogies" in the "Introduction: Pentateuch I," page 19. You may skip or scan the biblical text in this section.)

The Priestly author continues to provide continuity in the story. Up until this point, the primeval history concerned all nations. With the current genealogy, we move from Seth to Abram, who will eventually have his name changed to Abraham. Abraham will eventually be recognized as the father of the Israelite nation. The genealogy, like that of Noah, begins with Seth and ends with Abram, Nahor, and Haran, three sons of Terah. The theme of ending genealogies with three significant names follows the format of genealogies found in Genesis.

Once the story reaches Abram, it now becomes the story of the ancestors of Israel. The author repeats the names of the sons of Terah as Abram, Nahor, and Haran, the father of Lot. When Abram's wife, Sarai, is named, the author states that she was barren, setting the groundwork for a later miracle in the life of Abram. Haran dies before his father, Terah. Terah sets out from Ur of the Chaldeans with his grandson Lot, his son Abram, and Abram's wife. The planned destination was the land of Canaan, but when they reach Haran, they settle there. Terah dies at Haran.

Day 3: Abram's Call and Sojourn in Egypt (12)

God directs Abram to set out from his land, his relatives, and his father's house to a land that God promises to give him. With this, the saga of Abram begins. Most of his story comes from the Yahwist author, which makes it more ancient than some later stories. Leaving his land, relatives, and father's house could symbolize Abram's break from his past and his journey from paganism to the one God. Leaving was not his choice, but he was directed by God. His destination is also established by God, since he is to travel to the land God will show him. It seems that the blessing from the Lord for Abraham depends on his willingness to go to Canaan. God promises to bless those who bless Abram and curse those who curse him. Just as God confused the languages of the people and scatters them over the earth, God now promises that blessings will flow to all families of the earth through Abram.

Abram leaves Haran at the age of seventy-five and takes with him his wife, Sarai, and his brother's son, Lot, to the land of Canaan. In the land of Canaan, they travel to Shechem and then to Bethel, building an altar at each place. The dedication of the altars may symbolize God's claim over the pagan holy sites, and Abram's journey through Canaan may represent his claim on the land for his ancestors. Abram then journeyed to Negeb.

A story from the Yahwist author interrupts the story of Abram's journey to Negeb with a story about Abram and Sarai in Egypt. In this story, Abram and Sarai go to Egypt to avoid a famine that swept over the land. Abram tells Sarai to lie by saying that she is his sister. He feared that the Egyptians would kill him in order to take Sarai. The passage shows that Abram does not yet fully trust that the Lord would bless him and his offspring. When Pharaoh sees the beauty of Sarai, he takes her into his house. Abram prospered in Egypt because Pharaoh thought that Sarai was in the care of her brother Abram. When Pharaoh and his household become victims of a severe plague, Pharaoh discovers that Sarai is Abram's wife, and he rebukes Abram for lying. He has him sent away with his wife and all their belongings.

The story of the deception of Abram and Sarai will appear again in chapter 20. A similar story will also appear in a later story about Jacob and his wife Rebecca in 26:1–11. The duplication of events found in Genesis is not surprising since the stories were passed on through different traditions for a long period of time before someone wrote them down. There is also a subtle reference in the story to a later event in Genesis when the family of Jacob comes to Egypt to avoid a famine and centuries later leaves after a series of plagues afflict Pharaoh and the Egyptians (Genesis 45, 46, and Exodus 14).

Lectio Divina

Spend 8 to 10 minutes in silent contemplation of the following passage:

> We believe that the Lord is with us, but there are times when we lose confidence in God's presence and commit a sin to solve our situations. We can sometimes say within our hearts, "Lord, I trust you, but not in this situation." The good news about God is that God did not abandon Abram when Abram showed a lack of trust in God, who promised to be with him.

✠ *What can I learn from this passage?*

Day 4: Abram and Lot Part (13–14)

The story continues from verse 9 of the previous chapter. Abram returns to Negeb. The blessings God bestows on Abram become visible through the abundant wealth Abram accumulated. Abram's nephew, Lot, travels with Abram's family, and he too has become rich. Disputes were erupting between the herders of Abram's livestock and those of Lot, possibly over watering places that were valuable areas to shepherds. To avoid a family conflict and recognizing that they could not remain together, Abram and Lot agree to split from each other. Abram allows Lot to choose where he wishes to settle and Lot chooses to set up his tent on the Jordan plain near Sodom. This passage stresses the wickedness of Sodom.

After Lot leaves Abram, God directs Abram to look around at all the land in every direction. Just as Abram allowed Lot to lift up his eyes and look at the land he wanted, so God has Abram lift up his eyes to see the land God promised to give to his descendants. God's promise is that Abram's descendants will be as numerous as the dust. Here, God directs Abram to walk over this entire land, and Abram settles in Hebron where he builds an altar to the Lord. In this passage, Abram is fulfilling the command of God to "go to the land that I will show you" (12:1).

This is a difficult chapter that lacks extra-biblical support and which speaks about battles between various kingly factions. Four eastern kings join together and defeat five Canaanite kings from the Dead Sea region where Lot has settled. For twelve years, the Canaanite kings were subjected to an eastern coalition under the leadership of the Shemite king named Chedorlaomer. When the Canaanite kings revolt, the eastern kings crush the rebellion and capture Lot and his household. Then, Abram hears of the capture of Lot and musters an army of 318 men of his household, pursuing the retreating kings to the vicinity of Dan. In a nighttime assault, he wins the battle. He then pursues those fleeing to a city north of Damascus named Hobah. There, Abram recovers Lot and his possessions, including his women and children.

Upon Abram's return, Melchizedek, the king of Salem, brings him bread and wine. The reference to the king of Salem, written in Psalm 76:3 as Jerusalem and Mount Zion, says, "On Salem is God's tent, his shelter on Zion." This is the only place where Genesis associates a patriarch with Jerusalem and the only reference in the entire Torah to Jerusalem. Melchizedek blesses Abram, who offers Melchizedek a tenth of all he has. Then Abram refuses to return the captives to the king of Sodom who requests them, but not the supplies. Since he did not battle to be enriched by his victory, Abram returned the supplies, entrusting God to enrich him.

Lectio Divina

Spend 8 to 10 minutes in silent contemplation of the following passage:

Jesus tells us to love our neighbor as ourselves. The story of Lot and Abram offers an insight into love of neighbor. They certainly love each other, but in their wisdom, they realize that sharing the same land and water supply will jeopardize their relationship, so they decide to part from each other. Love of neighbor can mean that we make boundaries in order to respect them. Respecting both the rights of our neighbors and our own rights is essential. Love of neighbor demands that we attempt to live in peace with those who surround us—our brothers and sisters in Christ.

✠ *What can I learn from this passage?*

Day 5: Covenant with Abram (15)

A period of time passes and the word of the Lord speaks to Abram in a vision, directing Abram to have no fear because the Lord promises to be his shield. Abram asks what the Lord will give him since he has no offspring. It appears that his servant Eliezer will become his heir. The Lord promises Abram that he will have an heir from among his offspring and that his descendants will be as numerous as the stars. In this section, Abram put his faith in the Lord, an act of righteousness.

After Abram has received a promise of offspring as numerous as the stars, the message now turns its attention to the land. This passage comes from a different tradition than that found in the first six verses of this chapter. God leads Abram from Ur of the Chaldeans to this land that God has promised to him. When Abram asks how he will know that he will possess the land, God prepares for a covenant with Abram. God directs him to bring a heifer, a female goat, and a ram, all three years old, along with a turtledove and a small pigeon. Abram does so, cutting the animals in half with the exception of the birds. The cutting in half signified a commitment made in a treaty whereby a person is saying, "May the same happen to me if I break the treaty." The voice of the Lord offers a veiled prediction of the sojourn of the Israelites who will live in slavery in Egypt for four hundred years. The nation enslaving them will face God's wrath and they will leave the land with great wealth and return to the land where Abram resides. God promises Abram that he will be buried with his ancestors in peace, a significant and important prediction for people of Abram's era.

In the darkness, a smoking fire pot and a flaming torch passes between the divided carcasses as a sign of God's sealing of the covenant. God promises to give the land from the Wadi of Egypt to the Euphrates to Abram's descendants. The Wadi of Egypt was a dividing point between the Sinai desert and the area of the promise. But the land promised here is more than the Israelites later inhabited. The list of ten nations occupying this area is similar to other lists found in the Scriptures.

Lectio Divina

Spend 8 to 10 minutes in silent contemplation of the following passage:

Abram will have offspring as numerous as the stars, which is a foolish idea to a man and woman who are too old to have children. The foundation of Judaism and Christianity is that God is a God of history, a companion on the journey through life for all believers. The New Testament teaches that Jesus is our companion through life, and we seal that belief through the covenant of baptism. As long as Christ is with us, we can expect the impossible to happen, even when we are not aware of it or when it seems foolish.

✠ *What can I learn from this passage?*

Review Questions

1. What message can be understood from the passage where God grants permission for human beings to eat meat?
2. What is the relationship between Abram and Lot? Explain the significance of their relationship in Scripture.
3. Why did God choose Abram and make a covenant with him?

A Covenant With God

GENESIS 16—26

Abram fell face down and God said to him: "For my part, here is my covenant with you: you are to become the father of a multitude of nations. No longer will you be called Abram; your name will be Abraham" (17:3–5).

Opening Prayer (SEE PAGE 16)

Context

Part 1: Genesis 16—18:15 Hagar, Sarai's maidservant, gives birth to Ishmael, and Sarai makes Abram cast Hagar out. God finds Hagar and promises that she will bear a son who is to be named Ishmael. The Lord establishes a covenant with Abram and changes his name to Abraham. God will make Abraham the father of a great nation, and the covenant will continue to exist between Abraham and his descendants. As a sign of the covenant, every male shall be circumcised. God also changes the name of Sarai to Sarah. As the wife of Abraham, she will give rise to many nations. Ishmael, Abraham's son by Sarah's maidservant, will also birth a great nation. Abraham has visitors who predict that Sarah will have a son by the following year. When the Lord tells Abraham that Sodom is about to be destroyed, Abraham unsuccessfully tries to negotiate with God.

Part 2: Genesis 18:16—26 Lot and his family are saved from the destruction of Sodom and Gomorrah, but Lot's wife, upon disobeying the Lord's command, looks back and becomes a pillar of salt. Lot's two daughters, afraid that they will not have any children to carry on the line of Lot, get their father drunk and become pregnant by him. In his travels, Abraham again tells people that Sarah is his sister, and King Abimelech takes her. God threatens to kill Abimelech for taking Sarah. Abimelech rebukes Abraham and rewards him rather than have him as an enemy.

Abraham and Sarah have a son named Isaac. Sarah orders Abraham to cast out Hagar and her son Ishmael. God tests Abraham by commanding him to sacrifice his son Isaac, but at the last minute God supplies a ram in place of Isaac. Abraham sends one of his servants to find a wife for his son Isaac from among their kindred. Isaac marries Rebekkah who gives birth to twins, Esau and Jacob. A story similar to that of Abraham and Sarah takes place as Isaac and Rebekkah travel to another land to settle, and Isaac lies and says that she is his sister. The consequences are the same as that in the Abraham story.

PART 1: GROUP STUDY (GENESIS 16—18:15)

Read aloud Genesis 16—18:15.

16 Birth of Ishmael

When Sarai believed that she could bear no children, she follows a custom of her day which allowed (and in some cultures demanded) that a woman give her slave girl to her husband to bear a child. The woman who owned the slave girl had the right to adopt and claim the child of the slave as her own child. In ancient times, it was considered a disgrace for a woman not to bear a child within the first few years of marriage. And in the period in which Abram lived, infertility was blamed on the woman. Hagar is an Egyptian slave who will be maltreated by Sarai, just as the Egyptians will later mistreat the Israelites in Egypt. Hagar becomes pregnant and looks down on Sarai. When Sarai complains to Abram, Abram tells her that the slave girl is in her power, and she may do whatever she regards as right. Sarai mistreats Hagar to the point that Hagar has to flee.

In the desert, an angel of the Lord learns from Hagar that she is fleeing from Sarai. The angel directs Hagar to return and adds that she will bear a son whose offspring would be too numerous to count. The angel directs her to name the child Ishmael, which means "God has heard." The angel seems to predict that the offspring of Ishmael will live alongside the land promised to Abram, but not in it. Hagar names the angel as "God who sees," which could mean that God protects her or sees her suffering. There is an ancient belief that a person cannot look upon God and live. Although Hagar questions whether she has truly seen God and continues to live, she seems to believe that she has indeed seen the Lord face to face. The name of the well refers to the well of the one who sees. When Abram was eighty-six, Hagar bore him a son whom he named Ishmael.

17 Covenant of Circumcision

The Priestly author introduces the origin of the rite of circumcision. Abram has now reached the age of ninety-nine, significantly mentioned since it will show the miraculous powers of God acting in the life of Abram. God is identified as God the Almighty which could mean "God, the One of the Mountains." God establishes a covenant with Abram, promising that Abram will be a father of nations, and changes Abram's name to Abraham. But both names have the same meaning: "the father is exalted."

Since the author is writing from the perspective of one who already knows the history of Abraham's offspring, he places aspects of that history in God's words. God will create nations and kings from among the descendants of Abraham. Here, God agrees to be Abraham's God and the God of Abraham's descendants after him. In Abraham's day, the people of many nations had national gods and family gods. God is telling Abraham that the one true God will be his God and the one God of his descendants. God adds the promise of land to Abraham's descendants. Both the promise of a multitude of descendants and land were given earlier in chapter 15.

God informs Abraham that he and every male after him must be circumcised as a sign of the covenant. Abraham lived in a patriarchal society that viewed God as making covenants with the community through males. Circumcision was practiced in the ancient world as an initiation rite for males at puberty. When God moves the circumcision from puberty to eight days after birth, circumcision becomes a sign of a covenant between God and the descendants of Abraham instead of being an initiation rite. Besides all the descendants of Abraham, the male household slaves and those acquired with money must be circumcised. This covenant in the flesh will be a perpetual covenant. Males who are not circumcised will be excluded from the community, since they will be breaking the covenant.

In this passage, God also changes the name of Sarai to Sarah. Sarai and Sarah both mean "princess." She will give rise to great nations, and rulers of peoples will issue from her. Abraham laughs at the thought that a child can be born of a 100-year-old man and a ninety-year-old woman. The word "laughed" is also a Hebrew form of the name "Isaac."

Abraham pleads for God's favor for Ishmael, and God heeds Abraham's request, but the everlasting covenant shall exist between the descendants of Abraham and Sarah. God promises to make Ishmael the father of twelve chieftains and the father of a great nation. Even though Ishmael is the son of a slave girl, a case could be made for him having the right to the promise over Isaac, who is Abraham's second-born. When God finishes speaking, God departs. Abraham obeys the Lord, circumcising Ishmael, all his slaves—whether born in the house or acquired—every male member of his household, and he had himself circumcised.

18:1–15 Abraham's Visitors

In ancient times, hospitality demanded that a person sacrifice whatever is necessary for a guest. Abraham greets three visitors by bowing down and asking them to stay, eat, and drink. The men bathe their feet under the shade of the oak tree. The preparation of a meal begins, which includes baking bread, killing and cooking a calf, and setting them before the visitors with milk and curds, which would resemble a type of yogurt today. As a perfect host, Abraham does not sit to eat with them, but he waits on them as was expected in showing hospitality to guests.

When the visitors ask about Abraham's wife, he tells them that she was in the tent, which is where a woman would remain when guests arrived. One of the men predicts that upon their return the following year around the same time, Abraham and Sarah would have a son. Since Abraham and Sarah were old and Sarah had stopped having her menstrual periods, Sarah laughs at the thought that they would have sexual relations and bear a child. The Lord now speaks and asks Abraham why Sarah laughed. The Lord inquires whether there is anything too marvelous for the Lord to do. Sarah says that she did not laugh, but the Lord answers simply, "Yes you did."

Review Questions

1. Why would Sarah give her slave girl to her husband as a concubine?
2. Why does God seek a sign of the covenant only from males?
3. What is the significance of hospitality in ancient times?

Closing Prayer (SEE PAGE 16)

Pray the closing prayer now or after *lectio divina*.

Lectio Divina (SEE PAGE 9)

Relax your body and maintain a posture of prayer (back straight, eyes shut, feet flat on the floor). This exercise can take as long as you want, but in the context of this Bible study, 10 to 20 minutes should be sufficient.

The meditations that follow are provided only to help group participants use this prayer form, but note that *lectio* is intended to bring one to a place of prayerful contemplation where the Word of God speaks to the hearer from his or her heart. (See page 9 for further instruction.)

Birth of Ishmael (16)

God does not abandon the offspring of Hagar, the slave girl, but God writes straight with the crooked line and makes the offspring the father of a great nation, although not the offspring of God's promise of the land given to Abram. God invites us to follow a path on our journey through life, but we may take detours that force God, who loves us, to open up a new path before us. As Christians who realize how much Jesus has done to show us the love of God, we believe that God can write straight with the crooked lines of our lives.

✠ *What can I learn from this passage?*

Covenant of Circumcision (17)

For Christians, baptism has taken the place of circumcision as a means of committing oneself to the new covenant given through Jesus Christ. Merely to share in the sacrament of baptism and not to live up to its demands shows that a person misunderstands the sacrament, just as a Jewish circumcised male who does not love God is not living up to the standards of the covenant made between Abraham and God. Our faith demands that we view the sacrament of baptism not simply as a washing of the body but as a commitment of the heart.

✠ *What can I learn from this passage?*

Abraham's Visitors (18:1–15)

In Luke's Gospel, a woman who was a known sinner comes into the home of a Pharisee where Jesus is dining and washes Jesus' feet with her tears, dries them with her hair, kisses them, and anoints them. Jesus rebukes the Pharisee who invited him to dinner, saying that he gave Jesus no water to bathe his feet when he arrived, did not give him the usual kiss of greeting, and did not anoint his head with oil. The woman, whom they viewed as a sinner, showed hospitality to Jesus, while the Pharisee actually insulted Jesus with his lack of hospitality. Because of her hospitality, Jesus recognizes her great love and declares that her many sins are forgiven, while the Pharisee, who proved that he lacked love, would not have his sins forgiven. In 1 Peter we read that "love covers a multitude of sins" (4:8). In this case, love expressed through hospitality of the woman covered a multitude of sins. When Abraham showed hospitality to his visitors, they rewarded him with the promised child to be born of Sarah.

✠ *What can I learn from this passage?*

PART 2: INDIVIDUAL STUDY (GENESIS 18:16—26)

Day 1: Sodom and Gomorrah (18:16—19:29)

As the three men were leaving, the Lord considers whether or not to tell Abraham about the investigation of Sodom and Gomorrah, and the punishment in store for the evil committed in those cities. Since the Lord chose Abraham to be the father of a great and mighty nation and a source of blessing for all the nations of the world, the Lord entrusts Abraham with what is about to happen.

Abraham immediately knows the punishment in store for Sodom and Gomorrah if they are found to be guilty of grave evil. He becomes bold in the presence of the Lord and begins to negotiate, asking with a series of questions if the Lord would destroy the city if fifty, forty-five, forty, thirty, twenty, or ten righteous people are found in the city. In each case, the Lord promises to spare the city if a small number of people prove to be righteous. After agreeing to spare the city if ten righteous people can be found, the Lord leaves and Abraham returns home.

When the two angels reach Sodom, Lot, who is sitting by the gate and who does not recognize them as angels, bows down before them as Abraham did and invites them to stay with him, an important sign of hospitality. The Lord is no longer one of the visitors, since the author speaks only of two, not three, angels. Lot's invitation turns to pleading when the angels say they would pass the night in the town square. Lot prepares a banquet for them, and they dine.

Before bedtime, all the townsmen surround the house and demand that Lot bring out his visitors so that they could rape them. Lot goes out, closing the door behind him to protect his visitors, and offers his virgin daughters to the townsmen, thus fulfilling the obligations of hospitality demanded for the protection of visitors. The father had total ownership of his daughters and could do what he wished with them. The crowd ridicules Lot as an alien, that is, not a native of the area, trying to tell them what to do. They threaten to treat him worse than they would have treated his visitors. As the crowd presses closer, one of the visitors reaches out, pulls Lot into the house, and closes the door. The visitors then strike the men at the entrance with such a blinding light that they could not find the entrance.

The angels explain their mission to Lot and offer to allow him to escape with his wife, his daughters, and his sons-in-law. Lot's sons-in-law think he is joking and refuse to go. At dawn, the visitors urge Lot to leave, and when he tarries, they seize his hand and the hands of his wife and daughters and lead them outside the city. Lot asks that they allow him and his family to flee to Zoar, a small city in the area. When Lot reaches the city later in the day, God rains down sulfur on Sodom and Gomorrah. Lot's wife looks back and is turned into a pillar of salt. There are salt columns near the Dead Sea which resemble human forms. People, who look on these salt formations around the Dead Sea, would remember the story and the punishment Lot's wife received for not heeding the words of the angels.

The Priestly author returns the story to Abraham and makes him the reason for God's decision to spare Lot and his family. In the morning, Abraham rushes to the place where he stood before the Lord and sees the smoke rising over Sodom and Gomorrah and the whole region of the plain. The Priestly author states that God remembered Abraham and saved Lot. In the previous story, Lot was saved because of his hospitality to the two angels.

Lectio Divina

Spend 8 to 10 minutes in silent contemplation of the following passage:

Surprisingly, Abraham gives an example of prayer when he negotiates with God, attempting to change God's mind about the destruction of Sodom and Gomorrah. Many times, we pray as though we are negotiating with God. "God, if you will, you can heal my sinful (or suffering) relative (or friend)." God listens and considers, as God does with Abraham, and in the end, God acts with justice and mercy. God never says "No," but says, "I will do something."

✠ *What can I learn from this passage?*

Day 2: Deception of Lot's Daughters and Abraham (19:30—20)

Although Lot flees to Zoar, he fears remaining there, so he travels to the hill country and lives in a cave with his daughters. The daughters, apparently believing that everyone else in the world was killed in the overwhelming destruction of Sodom and Gomorrah, decide to have intercourse with their father so that Lot's posterity would continue. Losing one's line of descendants would be equivalent to losing one's mortality.

Lot's two daughters coax their father into drinking enough wine to make him drunk. On the first night, the firstborn has intercourse with her inebriated father and leaves his bed without him knowing it. The next night, the younger does the same. Both become pregnant with Lot's sons. The firstborn gives birth to a son whom she names Moab. The name Moab has a sound similar to the Hebrew expression "from my father." He becomes the father of the Moabites. The younger daughter names her child Ammon, which sounds similar to the Hebrew expression, "the son of my kin." He becomes the father of the Ammonites. The story reveals a family relationship between the Israelites and their two enemies, the Moabites and the Ammonites.

As a nomad with flocks in need of fertile areas, Abraham's journeys take him to Gerar, which makes him an alien in the land and leads him to fear that he would be killed by someone who desired to have his wife, Sarah. The story echoes an earlier story found in Genesis where Abraham directs his wife to claim that she is his sister (12:10–20). The similarity of these stories leads to the conclusion that the story of the wanderings of Abraham were told orally and that this is a single story passed on through different traditions and inserted in the story of Abraham by a later author. The author does not mention the ages of Abraham or Sarah, although it seems unlikely that Sarah is ninety years old, as stated in a previous episode.

Abimelech, the king of Gerar, believing that Sarah is Abraham's sister, takes her, but he does not touch her. God appears to Abimelech in a dream and tells him that he will die because he took another man's wife. Abimelech protests that he is innocent. Unknown to Abimilech, God kept him from touching Sarah. God tells Abimelech to return Sarah to Abraham so that

Abraham, who is here declared to be a prophet, can intercede for him and save him from death. This is the only passage in the Pentateuch where God refers to Abraham as a prophet. Although God admits that Abimelech took Sarah innocently, the threat of death still remains since it is the deed, not the intention, which is being judged.

The next day, Abimelech scolds Abraham for his deception. Abraham defends himself by claiming that Sarah is his half-sister, the daughter of his father but not of his mother. It is noteworthy that the prohibition against marrying one's half-sister did not exist until later in history. Abimelech gives animals and slaves to Abraham and allows him to settle anywhere on the land. He also tells Sarah that he is giving a thousand shekels of silver to her brother to preserve her honor and exonerate her before all. When Abraham intercedes for Abimelech, his household is restored to health, and his wife and maidservants can now bear children again.

Lectio Divina

Spend 8 to 10 minutes in silent contemplation of the following passage:

> The deception of Lot's daughters led to the birth of Israel's enemies who would become a thorn in the side of Israel. Abraham's deception almost led to the destruction of an innocent man and his family. Jesus tells his disciples to be "shrewd as serpents and simple as doves," (Matthew 10:16), but he does not tell them to be deceptive. Shrewdness does not include sinful deceptiveness.

✠ *What can I learn from this passage?*

Day 3: Birth of Isaac and the Covenant at Beer-sheba (21)

When Abraham showed hospitality to the angels, one of them said, "I will return to you about this time next year, and Sarah will have a son" (18:10). At the time set by the Lord, the child Isaac is born. Abraham, who was 100 years old when his son is born, circumcises the boy when he is eight days old. When Sarah sees Isaac and the son of the slave girl playing together, she tells Abraham to cast out the slave girl. This is the second time that Sarah has Hagar and her son sent away. Since Ishmael is also a son of Abraham, Abraham becomes distressed, but God promises Abraham that it will be through Isaac that his descendants will bear his name. God again pledges to make a nation from Ishmael.

The next morning, Abraham places the child on Hagar's back, gives her some bread and a skin of water, and sends her away. This passage comes from a different source than that found earlier in Genesis. Abraham was 100 years old when Isaac was born, and, according to an earlier story about the birth of Ishmael, he was eighty-seven years old when Ishmael was born (16:16). This would make Ishmael at least fourteen years old. He would walk alongside Hagar at that age and not be carried on her back. But the author of the present passage makes Isaac and Hagar about the same age.

After a period of time, Hagar and the child have no more water, so Hagar places him under a bush and goes away a distance so that she will not have to watch the child die. But God hears the cries of the child and repeats the prediction that Ishmael will become a great nation and provides water. The boy grows up in the wilderness and becomes a great bowman, and eventually his mother finds a wife for him from the land of Egypt.

Abimelech appears again, and this account becomes a continuation of the story found in chapter 20 of Genesis. Abraham tells Abimelech about his servants seizing a well dug by Abraham. Abimelech agrees with Abraham, and Abraham makes an offering as a seal of a covenant between Abraham and Abimelech. The passage notes that Abimelech will be a witness that the well was dug by Abraham. Abraham plants a tamarisk tree at Beer-sheba and calls upon the Lord God the Eternal, which was a reference to an ancient deity at the sanctuary at Beer-sheba before Abraham's time.

Lectio Divina

Spend 8 to 10 minutes in silent contemplation of the following passage:

The eucharistic celebration welcomes sinners with the hope that the grace of God will touch our hearts and bring about a conversion. During the liturgy, Jesus welcomes saints and sinners to join him in the meal, and Jesus, the bridegroom, celebrates with us.

✠ *What can I learn from this passage?*

Day 4: Abraham's Test (22)

The intriguing story of Abraham's willingness to sacrifice Isaac comes from the Eloist author, although there are a few verses attributed to the Yahwist author. As a test of Abraham's trust and faith in God, God tells him to take his son Isaac to the land of Moriah and to offer him as a burnt offering on one of the heights the Lord would point out to him. The test is twofold. Isaac is Abraham's only son from his wife, Sarah. If Abraham sacrifices Isaac, how will an old man like him, more than a hundred years old, have a son to fulfill God's promise that he would have offspring as numerous as the stars? The passage tells us that Isaac was a son whom Abraham loved. The love of Abraham for his son would make the sacrifice even more difficult. Abraham is directed to the land of Moriah, identified with Jerusalem in 2 Chronicles, where we read: "Then Solomon began to build the house of the Lord in Jerusalem, on Mount Moriah" (3:1). The morning after Abraham receives the Lord's command, he saddles a donkey, takes Isaac and two of his servants with him, and cuts the wood necessary for the burnt offering.

On the third day, when Abraham sees the place in the distance, he directs his servants to remain there with the donkey while he and his son move on to the place of worship. Isaac questions Abraham about a sheep for worship, but Abraham answers that God will provide. Some commentators believe that Abraham is hoping for God to provide something in the place of Isaac. Even if this is true, Abraham acts as though he is willing to sacrifice Isaac. As he raises his hand to kill Isaac, an angel of the Lord tells him not to touch the boy and declares that Abraham has proven his love for God in his willingness to sacrifice his only beloved son. God provides a ram caught in the thick brush by its horns. Abraham named the place "Yahweh-yireh," which people refer to as the mountain the Lord will provide.

Because Abraham passes this final crucial test, an angel's voice from heaven repeats God's promise to make Abraham's descendants as countless as the stars in the sky and the sands of the seashore. They will conquer their enemies and bring a blessing to all nations on earth. Abraham, his servants, and Isaac return home to Beer-sheba.

Upon his return, Abraham learns that his brother Nahor and his wife Michah gave birth to eight sons and that Nahor had four other sons from his concubine named Reumah. Later, Jacob, the son of Isaac, will have eight sons from his wives and four from his concubines. Rebekah, a granddaughter of Nahor and Michah, will later become the wife of Isaac.

Lectio Divina

Spend 8 to 10 minutes in silent contemplation of the following passage:

> Abraham loved and trusted God to the extent that he was willing to sacrifice his son born of Sarah. In doing this, Abraham and Isaac become a model of a future event. We read in John's Gospel, "For God so loved the world that he gave his only Son, so that everyone who believes in him might not perish but might have eternal life" (3:16). In the end, the Lord provided a ram in place of Abraham's son, but when Jesus was sacrificed, he endured the cross with no one to substitute for him. His death revealed how much God loves us.

✠ *What can I learn from this passage?*

Day 5: Isaac and Rebekah (23—25:18)

Sarah dies at the age of 127, and Abraham seeks to purchase land from the Hittites, but the owner of the particular site is a man named Ephron, who offers to give the land to Abraham as a gift. Abraham was not a native of the area and was considered an alien to the place. Ordinarily, aliens were not allowed to own land outside their own territory, but because of the blessings the Hittites experienced through Abraham, they allow him to own it. Abraham convinces Ephron to let him purchase the land for a considerable amount of money. Thus Ephron's field with the cave for the burial now belongs to Abraham. With the purchase of land, the promise that this land would be given to Abraham's descendants would be fulfilled. This was only part of the land promised, since more will be taken with conquests led by Joshua and gained during the reign of David.

Since Abraham is living in the land of the Canaanites, he sends a trusted servant to his homeland to find a wife for Isaac. He directs the servant to place his hand under the thigh of Abraham and take an oath that he will take a wife from among his own relatives and not from the among the Canaanites. Taking an oath by placing one's hand under the thigh was most likely linked with the idea that children came from their father's thigh. It may have been thought that the one making the oath would abide by it or suffer the punishment of becoming infertile. Once the servant finds a woman to be a wife for Isaac, he is to bring her back with him. If she refuses to come with the servant, then the servant is released from his oath. The servant travels to Nahor.

The servant sets for himself a sign to show that the Lord has chosen a woman as wife for Isaac. When he is standing by a well and asks for a drink from a woman's jug, and she agrees to give him water and to provide water for his camels, he will take this as a sign that God has chosen this woman as wife for Isaac. Rebekah is the first woman at the spring. She gives him water and volunteers to water his camels. She informs him that she is the daughter of Bethel, who is the son of Micah and Abraham's brother Nahor. He offers her a gold nose-ring and two gold bracelets, gifts which are signs that a marriage is expected to take place, since God pointed out Rebekah to the servant. He asks her to take him and his companions to her father's home so they may rest for the night, and he repeats the story about his quest to the family. Although the family would like Rebekah to remain with them for ten days, the servant wishes to return immediately to Abraham. They decide to ask Rebekah who agrees that she will go with him.

Isaac apparently knows the reason for the journey and is out walking when he sees the camels returning. When the servant tells Isaac all that has happened, Isaac takes Rebekah into his mother's tent and takes her as his wife. He loved her and found comfort in her after the death of his mother.

The author lists all the descendants of Abraham, thus ending the story of Isaac and Rebekah. Abraham takes another wife named Keturah who gives birth to twelve sons for Abraham. Most notable on this list is Midian, who becomes the father of the Midianites, who were traders. Since Abraham had so many sons, he had to designate the son who would receive the inheritance, so he gives all he owns to Isaac. During his lifetime, he gave gifts to his other sons and sent them away from his son Isaac, apparently to establish Isaac as the true and only heir.

Abraham dies at the age of 175. Significantly it was both Isaac and Ishmael who buried him next to his wife, Sarah, in the cave of Machpelah, in the field of Ephron, the field Abraham bought from the Hittites. After the death of Abraham, Isaac is blessed by God as Abraham was.

The story concludes with the genealogy of Ishmael, who lived 137 years (25:12–18). In an earlier chapter in Genesis, an angel of the Lord tells Hagar that her son Ishmael shall encamp alongside his kindred (16:12).

Lectio Divina

Spend 8 to 10 minutes in silent contemplation of the following passage:

In our society, we may miss the many ways God acts in our midst. Unlike the servant of Abraham who clearly saw God's hand in the choice of Rebekah, we do not see the hand of God at work with such clarity. A famous saying tells us that we should pray as though everything depends on God and work as though everything depends on us. God works with us, not for us.

✠ *What can I learn from this passage?*

Day 6: Birth of Esau and Jacob (25:19—26)

The conception and birth of Esau and Jacob foreshadows the events that will take place after the birth of the twin brothers. The typical infertility portion of the story leads Isaac to pray for his wife. When God answers Isaac's prayer, the children jostle with each other in Rebekah's womb. The Lord reveals that there are two nations warring within her, and that the older will serve the younger.

At the time of birth, the first child to emerge was reddish and hairy, so they named him Esau. Esau was another name for Edom, also referring to the country south of Moab where Esau's descendants lived. Its reddish sandstone led to its name meaning the red country. Hairy in Hebrew is a reference to Seir, another name for Edom. Later in Genesis, we will read that Esau settled in the highlands of Seir (36:8). The second twin emerges gripping Esau's heel, so he receives the name Jacob, which is a play on the Hebrew word for heel. Isaac was sixty years old when his sons are born.

The difference between both sons becomes even more evident as they grow up. Esau, the favorite of Isaac, becomes a skilled hunter who loves the open country, while Jacob, the favorite of Rebekah, remains among the tents. One day, when Jacob was cooking stew, Esau comes in and asks for some of "that red stuff," declaring that he was famished. Jacob negotiates with Esau who, under oath, willingly sells his birthright to Jacob for some bread and stew. At the time, Esau had little regard for his right as firstborn.

In chapters 12 and 20 of Genesis, we encountered similar stories about Abraham and Sarah saying that they were brother and sister because Abraham feared that someone would kill him to take his wife (12:10–20, and 20:1–18). A third story of lying about one's wife takes place in the life of Isaac and Rebekah. It follows again, that since the stories were passed on orally for generations before they were committed to writing, some of them were found in various traditions to be the same story with slight variations. In this case, the story includes Isaac and Rebekah instead of Abraham and Sarah, and the characters of the story are Abimelech and others who are mentioned in chapter 20 with a very similar type of story.

When a famine strikes the land, Isaac goes to Abimelech, the king of the Philistines in Gerar. The Lord tells Isaac not to go to Egypt, but to go where the Lord directs him. The Lord directs Isaac to sojourn in the area where he is, and God renews with Isaac the promise God made to Abraham. The renewal of the promise is based on the obedience of Abraham to the Lord's commands.

When Isaac settles in Gerar as Abraham did in his story of deception, he tells the people that Rebekah is his sister. One day, when Abimelech looks out the window and sees Isaac fondling Rebekah, he confronts Isaac, knowing now that Rebekah is his wife. He reprimands Isaac, saying that anyone could have laid with Rebekah and brought guilt on all of them. Abimelech commands the people under penalty of death not to maltreat this man or woman.

When the Philistines saw how blessed Isaac had become with an abundant crop, an increase in flocks and herds, and a great work force, they become resentful of him. They plug the wells that Abraham dug. Water was scarce and valuable in the area, and the ones who had the water actually controlled the land. Abimelech asks Isaac to move, apparently because Isaac's flock and family had become too numerous to be supported by the land and the Philistines who lived on the land.

Isaac moves to the Wadi Gerar and reopens the wells dug by Abraham's household. A dispute arises between the shepherds of Gerar and Isaac's shepherds over the rights to the water. He names the well Esek, which means "quarrel." He digs another well and they argue over that well, so he names it Sitnah, which means opposition. So he moves on and digs another well, but they do not argue over it, so he names it Rehoboth, meaning wide spaces. Here Isaac declares that with ample room, they will flourish in the land.

Isaac travels to Beer-sheba, where the Lord appears to him declaring that for the sake of Abraham, the Lord would be with him to bless him and multiply his offspring. Isaac builds an altar there and invokes the Lord by name. Abimelech, recognizing how the Lord blessed Isaac, comes to him seeking to make a covenant with him whereby the two sides would not mistreat each other. The morning after eating and drinking together, they exchange oaths. When Isaac's servants inform him that they reached water in the well they were digging, he names it Shibah, which was a play on Hebrew words to express an oath. Esau married two women who would become a source of bitterness to Isaac and Rebekah.

Lectio Divina

Spend 8 to 10 minutes in silent contemplation of the following passage:

Abraham had his struggles and fears, and now Isaac has his. Christians know that Jesus never promised his followers that being disciples would lead to an easy life. He told his disciples, "If they persecuted me, they will also persecute you" (John 15:20). In Mark's Gospel, Jesus says that those who wish to come after him must pick up their cross and follow him (8:34). Living close to God brings much joy into life, but it also challenges us to remain faithful when difficulties or disappointments occur.

✠ *What can I learn from this passage?*

Review Questions

1. What is significant about the destruction of Sodom and Gomorrah?
2. Why does Abraham have to lie about Sarah being his sister?
3. Why is the story of Isaac the shortest of the patriarch's stories?

From Jacob to Joseph

GENESIS 27–38

"What is your name?" the man asked. He answered, "Jacob." Then the man said, "You shall no longer be named Jacob, but Israel, because you have contended with divine and human beings and you have prevailed" (32:28–29).

Opening Prayer (SEE PAGE 16)

Context

Part 1: Genesis 27—28 When Isaac was not able to see well because of his old age, he tells Esau to hunt and prepare a meal for him. Isaac intended to bless Esau, but Jacob, with the prompting and help of Rebekah, tricks the nearly blind Isaac into thinking that he was Esau, and Isaac blesses Jacob. Rebekah, knowing Esau wanted to kill Jacob as a result of the deception, persuades Isaac to send Jacob to her brother, Laban, to find a wife among his kinfolk. Jacob stops on his journey to rest, and he dreams of a stairway to heaven with angels going up and down. The Lord stood by him, affirming that he has received the promise given to Abraham.

Part 2: Genesis 29—38 Jacob loves Rachel, a daughter of Laban, and agrees to work for him for seven years in exchange for permission to marry Rachel. After seven years, Laban tricks Jacob into partying and later consummating his marriage with Leah, the older daughter of Laban. When Jacob discovers the deception the next morning, he rebukes Laban. Laban agrees to allow Jacob to marry Rachel also if he is willing to work seven more years. Jacob then marries Rachel. Rachel, unable at first to have children, gives her slave girl to Jacob to bear children. Leah gives birth to children, but when she no longer conceives, she gives her maidservant named Zilpah to Jacob so that she could claim more children for herself. Jacob eventually has two children from Rachel. Jacob has twelve sons and some unnamed daughters, but the author mentions his daughter Dinah who is later raped. Jacob escapes from serving Laban with his household and livestock, but Laban catches up with Jacob and they establish an agreement between them.

Before meeting with Esau, Jacob sends envoys ahead to appease his brother, whom he has not seen for many years. The night before he was to meet with Esau, Jacob camps alone and wrestles all night with a man who is later identified as an angel of God. Jacob and Esau meet in a friendly manner.

PART 1: GROUP STUDY (GENESIS 27—28)

Read aloud Genesis 27—28.

27:1-45 Jacob's Deception

The Yahwist author tells an amusing story of Jacob tricking Isaac into giving him Esau's blessing. As an old man whose eyesight is failing, Isaac directs Esau to go and kill some game and to bring it to him to eat so that he can give his blessing to Esau. The cunning Rebekah overhears Isaac's words, and she directs Jacob to get two goats from the flock. She prepares a meal she knows Isaac will enjoy and clothes Jacob in Esau's clothing; and she puts skin of the goats on Jacob's hands and the back of his neck. Jacob fears that if the father discovered the deception, Jacob would be cursed instead of blessed, but Rebekah says that Jacob should let any curse against him fall on her.

Jacob goes to his father, who was surprised that the meal was prepared so quickly. He tells his son to come closer to feel if he is really Esau. When he feels Jacob, he says that the voice is Jacob's, but the hands are Esau's.

Then Jacob serves the meal to Isaac and afterward gives him wine to drink. Isaac bids Jacob to come closer so that he may kiss him. When Jacob does so, Isaac recognizes the smell of the field on Esau's clothing which Jacob was wearing. He blesses Jacob, asking God to give him the dew of the heavens, signifying the rain watering the grain and wine and to make the earth fertile to bring forth an abundance of fruit. He adds, "May people serve you, and nations bow down to you," and continues with the most devastating blow against Esau, "Be master of your brothers, and may your mother's sons bow down to you" (27:29).

When Esau arrives with the meal, Isaac realizes that he was tricked into giving the blessing to Jacob. Once he has given the blessing, he cannot take it back or give it to someone else. Esau responds that Jacob is well-named since he has supplanted Esau twice. The phrase "he has supplanted me" is a Hebrew play on words for Jacob. Esau begs for a blessing, and Isaac gives a blessing in reverse of what he gave Jacob. He will live far from the fertile earth and from the rain from heaven. He will live by the sword and will serve his brother.

An angry Esau plans to kill Jacob after the mourning period for their father, who has not yet died. Apparently Esau does not want to anger his father, so he cannot carry out his plan until his death. Rebekah hears about Esau's plan to kill Jacob and warns her son to flee to her brother Laban in Haran and to remain with him until his brother's rage calms down. She says that when Esau forgets what Jacob did and forgives him, she will send for him.

27:46—28:9 Jacob Sent to Laban

Rebekah complains to Isaac that she would have no reason for living if Jacob should marry a Hittite woman. Isaac summons Jacob and forbids him to marry a Canaanite woman. Isaac then sends Jacob to the home of Bethuel where he may choose a wife from among the daughters of Rebekah's brother, Laban. Again Isaac blesses Jacob and prays that God would bless him and make him fertile so that he would become a large nation on the land promised to Abraham. Jacob went to live with Laban.

When Esau heard his father bless Jacob and tell him that he should not marry a Canaanite woman, Esau recognized how displeasing the Canaanite women were to his father, so Esau decided to marry a daughter of Ishmael. Esau seems to make one mistake after the other. He marries outside the family line that has received Abraham's blessing from God.

28:10–22 Jacob's Dream at Bethel

On his journey to Haran, Jacob stops to rest for the night, placing a stone under his head to sleep there. The author states that Jacob stopped "at a certain place." The Hebrew for a certain place often connotes a sacred site. Jacob is not yet aware of the sacredness of the site where he is resting which was a sacred site from the time of Abraham. In chapter 12 of Genesis, the author tells us that Abraham, who was also on a journey to Haran, set up a sacred altar at Bethel when God promised to give land to his descendants (12:7).

Jacob dreams of a stairway with its base on the ground and its top reaching to the heavens and angels going up and down it. Some translations use the word "ladder" instead of "stairway" in this passage, but stairway seems more correct. The Lord stands beside him and informs him that the Lord is the God of Abraham and Isaac. God will give the land where Jacob is lying to him and his descendants. God promises to be with Jacob and to protect him wherever he goes, bringing him back to this land. The Lord promises never to leave Jacob until all that the Lord promised would be fulfilled.

When Jacob awakens, he declares, "Truly, the Lord is in this place and I did not know it." He calls the place sacred, seeing it as the house of God, the gateway to heaven. Jacob takes the stone from under his head and sets it up as a sacred pillar and pours oil on it. A sacred pillar could be a stone of any size and shape intended for sacred purposes. This pillar designated the place as sacred to God. Jacob names the place Bethel, meaning the "house of God," whereas the former name had been Luz. He made a vow that if the Lord provided food and clothes for his journey, and if he came back safely to his father's house, the Lord would be his God. He is anticipating his return to the home of Isaac and wondering about his reception by Esau. Jacob promises to return a tenth of all the Lord gives him back to the Lord.

Review Questions

1. Why does God allow deceptions such as Jacob's to take place with no negative judgment being made by God?

2. What is your impression of Esau?

3. Why does Isaac want Jacob to marry from among their clan?

Closing Prayer (SEE PAGE 16)

Pray the closing prayer now or after *lectio divina*.

Lectio Divina (SEE PAGE 9)

Relax your body and maintain a posture of prayer (back straight, eyes shut, feet flat on the floor). This exercise can take as long as you want, but in the context of this Bible study, 10 to 20 minutes should be sufficient.

The meditations that follow are provided only to help group participants use this prayer form, but note that *lectio* is intended to bring one to a place of prayerful contemplation where the Word of God speaks to the hearer from his or her heart. (See page 9 for further instruction.)

Jacob's Deception (27:1–45)

A blessing from one's father with the Semitic tradition was more than wishing a person well. It was belief that the spirit of the father was in some manner passed on to the son. Jacob was chosen by God to carry on the heritage and traditions of Abraham and Sarah. In the New Testament, Jesus told his disciples, "It was not you who chose me, but I who chose you ...."(John 15:16). Every baptized Christian is the chosen one, the one called to carry on the heritage and traditions of Christ.

✠ *What can I learn from this passage?*

Jacob Sent to Laban (27:46—28:9)

Although the offspring of Abraham lived among pagans, they needed the support of their kinsmen to remain faithful to the one true God. Support and example have a great effect on our lives. Just as Jacob had to live among his kinfolk, so Christians need the support of faithful Christians. Our call

---

is to learn from one another and also to be examples to one another. We belong to the family of Christ.

✠ *What can I learn from this passage?*

Jacob's Dream at Bethel (28:10–22)

A man who was nearly killed when he fell from a second-story window and broke some bones said to a friend that he thought he was going to travel the stairway to heaven, meaning that he thought he was going to die. Jacob had a dream about a stairway to heaven, but it was not a dream about death, but a dream about life. Angels were going up and down, showing a link between heaven and earth. God is with us each day of our life and is our stairway to heaven.

✠ *What can I learn from this passage?*

PART 2: INDIVIDUAL STUDY (GENESIS 29—38)

Day 1: Jacob, His Wives, and His Sons (29—30:24)

When Jacob arrives at a well covered with a large stone, he sees three flocks of sheep huddled near the well. The shepherds informed Jacob that they would be able to roll the stone back when all the shepherds had assembled. They say that they come from Haran. Jacob asks how Laban, the son of Nahor, was fairing. They told him that Laban was well and that his daughter, Rachel, was just arriving with Laban's sheep.

When Rachel arrives and Jacob sees her, he goes up and easily rolls back the stone from the mouth of the well. Jacob's astonishing burst of strength testifies to his enthusiasm in meeting Rachel, and it reminds the reader that this is an idealized story of Jacob and his family. Jacob waters Laban's sheep and, greeting Rachel with a kiss, he weeps as he introduced himself as Rebekah's son. Rachel runs to tell Laban, who rushes out to meet and embrace Jacob.

Laban has two daughters, Leah the elder and Rachel. Jacob offers to work for Laban for seven years to marry Rachel. Laban agrees, and after seven years, Laban holds a wedding banquet. At nightfall, Laban takes his daughter Leah to Jacob, who unwittingly consummates the marriage with her. The author tells us that Rachel was beautiful, but Leah has "dull eyes," which could simply mean that she was not pretty. When Jacob awakens in the morning, he discovers that Laban has tricked him into marrying Leah. The act of consummation was considered the marriage commitment.

Jacob asks Laban, "How could you do this to me?" Laban defends his action by saying that it was not the custom to give a younger daughter in marriage before the firstborn. If a younger daughter marries before her older sibling, it brings shame to the elder daughter. Laban follows the custom of the era and saves his older daughter from disgrace. Laban directs Jacob to finish the bridal week with the promise that he would give Rachel to him in exchange for seven more years of service. At the end of the bridal week, Jacob receives Rachel as his second wife. Laban assigns a maidservant named Zipah to Leah and another named Bilhah to Rachel. Jacob consummates his marriage with Rachel and loves her more than he loved Leah. Then he serves Laban for another seven years.

The family of Abraham sees the hand of God in every event of life. The author tells us that when the Lord saw that Leah is unloved, he makes her fruitful while Rachel remains infertile. Leah bears Reuben, whose name means that the "Lord saw my misery; surely now my husband will love me" (29:32). She bears a second child and names him Simeon, which means "he heard." Her third son is named Levi, which means "he will become attached." She then bears her fourth and final son and names him Judah, meaning "I give thanks, praise."

Rachel gives her maidservant to Jacob so that she could have children "born on my knees." The expression is a symbol whereby the child is placed on the knees of the woman to indicate a valid adoption. Bilhah gives birth to a child whom Rachel, the valid adoptive parent, names Dan, which means "he has vindicated." Bilhah gives birth to a second child, and Rachel names him Naphtali, which means "contest" or "struggle."

When Leah realizes that she is no longer bearing children, she gives her maidservant Zipah to Jacob as a wife. Zipah bears a child whom Leah names Gad, which means "what good luck." Then Leah's maidservant bears a second son named Asher, which means "it is my good fortune."

One day Reuben brought some mandrakes to Leah. Mandrakes were considered some type of potion believed to help with conception. Rachel wants some of the mandrakes, and in exchange she allows Jacob to have intercourse with Leah that night. That night, Leah bears a fifth son whom she names Issachar, which means "I have hired you." Leah conceives a son again, and she named him Zebulun, which means "he will honor me." After this, she bears a daughter named Dinah. God then remembers Rachel and makes her fruitful. She bears a son whom she names Joseph, which means "God has removed my disgrace."

Lectio Divina

Spend 8 to 10 minutes in silent contemplation of the following passage:

> The tribes of Israel are coming into being with the guidance of God and the strengths and weaknesses of human nature. The deceptions of Jacob and Laban and the jealousies of Jacob's wife lead to the birth of twelve sons. The story tells us that God still has concern for creation. God is present in some manner as a companion and guide, and as one who invites; truly points to ponder.

✠ *What can I learn from this passage?*

Day 2: Jacob and Laban in Conflict (30:25—32:3)

After Rachel gives birth to Joseph, Jacob asks Laban to allow him to go to his own region and land with his wives and children. When Laban asks what he can give Jacob, Jacob asks that Laban allow him to go through his flock and remove every dark animal from among the lambs and every spotted or speckled goat. Jacob says that this would satisfy his wages. In this way, Laban could tell whether Jacob stole any sheep or goat by looking for light or unspotted animals among his flock.

Laban easily agrees, since sheep were ordinarily white and goats were ordinarily dark and not spotted or speckled. Laban, however, removes all the streaked and spotted he-goats and all those with some white on them as well as every dark lamb and puts them in the care of his sons. Afterward, he moved a three-day journey away from Jacob.

Jacob, as devious as Laban, sets shoots that he cut and pealed from trees in the water trough where the animals come to drink. He peels white stripes in them. The animals mate by the shoots and give birth to streaked, speckled, and spotted young. The sheep he made face the streaked or completely dark animals of Laban. Thus, he produces flocks of his own which he does not put with those of Laban. Because of this, Jacob prospers with large flocks, servants, camels, and donkeys. This story was based on a false assumption of the day that an animal's conception was influenced by what it saw.

Laban's sons accuse Jacob of taking all that belonged to their father, and Jacob realizes that Laban himself no longer values him. The Lord commands Jacob to return to the land of his ancestors, where he was born. Jacob conveys his belief to Rachel and Leah that Laban has changed his attitude toward him, explaining how he made sure that the speckled and streaked animals would prosper. The daughters remark that Laban has stolen from them also, taking all the wealth that rightfully belonged to them. Since all the wealth used by Laban actually belongs to them, they bid Jacob to do whatever the Lord tells him. Jacob puts his entire family on camels with the intention of going to his father, Isaac. Laban was away shearing sheep when Jacob flees with his wives, children, and all his wealth. On the third day, Laban receives word that Jacob has fled, and after seven days, catches up with them. Laban receives a vision from God telling him to take care not to say anything to Jacob.

When Laban reaches Jacob, he speaks as though he is innocent and demands that Jacob convey why he deceived him and carried off his daughters like prisoners. Acting like a caring father and loving grandfather, he reproves Jacob for not allowing him to even kiss his daughters and grandchildren.

Jacob admits that he feared Laban and believed that Laban would take his daughters away from him by force. When Laban asks why Jacob stole his family gods, Jacob denies it, saying that, with everyone looking on, he would not allow the one who took it to live. After Laban searches everywhere except Rachel's saddlebags, for she excuses herself from being moved since she claimed that she was having her period, he did not find his family gods. Jacob now becomes angry with Laban and lists all the good deeds and more that he had done for him. He then accuses Laban of allowing him to leave with the daughters and the flock only because he fears the God of Abraham and Isaac. When he says that Laban let him go due to "the Fear of Isaac," he means that Laban fears the God of Isaac, Jacob's father.

Laban seeks to make a covenant with Jacob. The passage becomes confusing, since the editor is mingling the Yahwist tradition with the Eloist tradition. The Yahwist tradition speaks more frankly, while the Eloist tradition seeks to support the hero of the story, who, of course, is Jacob. For that reason, we read that Jacob took a stone and set it up as a sacred pillar, which would have sufficed, but then we read that he had his kinsmen gather stones to make a mound. They ate there as a sign of agreement, and Laban gave it one name while Jacob called it Gileed, and also Mizpah, which is a town in Galilee. The word means "may the Lord keep watch."

The covenant means that they may not pass this pillar or mound with hostile intentions. Laban invokes the God of Abraham and the God of Nahor, the God of their father, to judge between them. Jacob then takes the oath by the God (Fear) of his father Isaac. He offers a sacrifice on the mountain and invites his kinsmen to again share in a meal. After the meal, they spend the night on the mountain. The story of Laban comes to an end the next morning as he kisses his daughters and grandchildren and returns to his home.

Jacob continues his journey and encounters God's angel, who leads him to exclaim that this was God's encampment. The scene recalls Jacob's journey to meet Laban for the first time. He stops to rest at Bethel, and at that time, after having a visitation from the Lord in a dream, he exclaimed that this was the Lord's place, the gateway to heaven (Genesis 28:17). Jacob names the encampment of God a Mahanaim, which means "two camps," which could be an allusion to the two camps that Jacob will later create to protect at least half of his wealth.

Lectio Divina

Spend 8 to 10 minutes in silent contemplation of the following passage:

Laban has been taking advantage of Jacob and Jacob's wives, yet he sees himself as a victim, asking Jacob why he has deceived him. The story shows Laban's inability to see his own faults. He views the fault of Jacob against him as unforgivable. Jesus, knowing human nature, once said, "Why do you notice the splinter in your brother's eye, but do not perceive the wooden beam in your own eye" (Matthew 7:3). It is much easier to see how another has hurt us than to see how we are hurting the other person.

✠ *What can I learn from this passage?*

Day 3: Envoys to Esau (32:4—33:20)

The Yahwist author presents the first part of this passage (32:1–13). Hoping to find peace with his brother, Jacob sends messengers ahead to Esau, who previously vowed to kill him for stealing his birthright. Jacob has his messengers report about his stay with Laban and his present wealth of oxen, donkeys, sheep, and servants. When the messengers return and tell Jacob that his brother is coming with 400 men, Jacob becomes frightened and splits his household and animals into two camps, so that if Esau attacked one, the other would be able to escape.

At this point, the Eloist author adds to the story. The next morning, Jacob shrewdly seeks to reward Esau little by little with many gifts of goats, sheep, camels, cows, and donkeys, and he separates them from each other into herds, so that one herd will arrive a short while after the other. The servants who meet Esau with each herd are to tell him that the herds are gifts from Jacob, who is coming. Jacob then moves his family across the river, including his wives, the maidservants, his eleven children (more perhaps, since female children such as Dinah were not ordinarily counted), and whatever belonged to him. This left him alone on one side of the river.

There was a tale concerning a spirit who guarded the crossing, a tale that could have some connection with the Yahwist story of Jacob, who now wrestles here with an unknown man throughout the night. In the morning, the man strikes Jacob's hip and dislocates the socket of the hip. Jacob refuses to free the man until the man blesses him, but instead of a blessing, the man changes Jacob's name to Israel. This change of name signifies a change of status for Jacob. Before the name change, Jacob, which signifies Jacob as the "supplanter" because he supplanted Esau's birthright as the son of the inheritance, is now recognized by his descendants as the ancestor of the Chosen People.

Jacob gives the place the name "Peniel," which is a variant of "the face of God," and Jacob exclaims that he has seen the face of God and lived. The man with whom Jacob wrestled is now identified as the Lord. It was believed that anyone who saw the face of God would die. Since Jacob limped because of the encounter, the author says that is why, to this day, the Israelites do not eat the hip socket of animals (32:33). This is the only place in Israelite history where the prohibition to eating the hip socket of animals is found.

Jacob approaches Esau in a subservient manner, bowing seven times before reaching him. Esau, surprisingly, runs to meet Jacob, embraces him, kisses him, and weeps. Jacob then points out his large family to Esau, possibly with the intention of showing that God has indeed blessed him. Esau attempts to refuse the gifts Jacob has sent ahead, saying that he has plenty, but Jacob persuades him to accept the gifts. Jacob offers Esau a high form of praise when he says that seeing him is like seeing the face of God.

After these initial beginnings, Esau and Jacob appear to play a game of mastery with each other, as Esau offers to take the lead position with Jacob following. Jacob's humble manner of approaching Esau may have made Esau believe that Jacob will be subservient to him, but Jacob makes the excuse that the children are too young and the herds that are nursing could die if driven too quickly and far. He urges Esau to return to his home at Seir with the intent of meeting him there. Esau offers some of his people to assist Jacob, but Jacob refuses. After Esau leaves him, Jacob goes in a different direction to a town named Succoth where he built a home and made booths for his livestock. The name Succoth has the same sound in Hebrew as the name for booths.

He soon left Succoth to cross the Jordan and enter the land of the Canaanites, settling at Shechem in sight of the city. His ancestor Abraham dedicated an altar at this site, as Jacob would do, and Jacob buys the plot of ground. When Jacob builds the altar there, "he...invoked El, the God of Israel" (33:20).

Lectio Divina

Spend 8 to 10 minutes in silent contemplation of the following passage:

At the center of the story of Jacob's return to his brother is the night Jacob wrestles with an angel. The angel, whom Jacob later identifies as the Lord, changes Jacob's name to Israel, because he contended with divine and human beings and has prevailed. This episode touches the lives of all of us who must contend with the divine by faith and our senses and emotions—our humanity. We wrestle with our desire to love God and many of the temptations of daily life.

✠ *What can I learn from this passage?*

Day 4: The Revenge of Dinah's Brothers (34—35:29)

Although Jacob may have had several daughters, the only one named was Dinah, most likely because of the story that follows. Shechem, a son of Hamor the Hivite, rapes Dinah and falls in love with her. He tells his father to get this young woman for him to have as a wife. When Dinah's brothers learn what happened, they become outraged, but Hamor appeals to Jacob and his sons to allow intermarriage between the men and women of both tribes. In repayment, he would allow them to settle anywhere they wished.

The brothers say they cannot allow their daughters to marry those who are uncircumcised, and they refuse to allow this marriage of Dinah and Shechem unless all the men of the city are circumcised. Hamor and his son convince his own people to accept circumcision in order to unite with the family of Jacob. He presents as a motive his intent to deceive Jacob's family. Once they start to share all their possessions, the Hittites intend to make the Israelites possessions their own. All males accept circumcision, and on the third day, when the men of the city were still helplessly in pain, Simon and Levi, brothers of Dinah, massacre all the males with their sword. The other sons of Jacob sack the city and take the livestock, wealth, children, women, and personal belongings.

Jacob rebukes Simeon and Levi, telling them that they have made him vile in the eyes of the Canaanites and the Perizzites. He warns that if these people unite, they will annihilate all of Jacob's household and his belongings. The brothers deflect the rebuke by asking if they should accept that their sister is treated like a prostitute. When a woman is violated as Dinah was, it falls on the brothers to avenge her.

The story of Dinah is followed by one similar to earlier stories that most likely have their origin in a different tradition. The following story has many features that come from the Priestly tradition. Jacob receives a message from God to revisit Bethel and build an altar there to God, who appeared to him when he fled from Esau. Jacob tells those of his household and all traveling with him to prepare for the journey by ridding themselves of all images of foreign gods, purifying themselves, and changing their clothes. The journey becomes a type of pilgrimage. The author speaks of a great terror that befalls the surrounding towns, perhaps because they knew of the previous slaughter of the Shechemites.

Jacob and his people build an altar at El-Bethel. The "El" refers to "God." This is the God of Bethel who was revealed to Jacob when he was fleeing from his brother. When Deborah, Rebekah's nurse, dies, she is buried beneath an oak tree near Bethel in a place they name Allon-bacuth, which means the "oak of weeping."

In this Priestly narrative, God appears to Jacob, blesses him, and changes his name from Jacob to Israel, as was done previously in a story taken from the Yahwist tradition. The Priestly author gives no reason for the change of a name. God tells Jacob to be fruitful and multiply, but this seems unlikely at this point since Jacob already had eleven sons. God again promises to give the land promised to Abraham and Isaac to Jacob's descendants. The Priestly author repeats Jacob's action of setting up a sacred stone pillar, making an offering, pouring oil on it, and naming the land Bethel.

Rachel dies giving birth to a son. Due to the affliction she suffers in giving birth, she names the child Benoni, which means "child of affliction or sorrow." Jacob, now referred to as Israel, changes the child's name to the more exalted name of Benjamin, which means "son of my right hand," the place of honor. According to the author, Rachel, the favorite wife of Jacob, was buried on the road to Ephrath. A later author added a note that the place is now called Bethlehem, which would place it south of Jerusalem. Jeremiah the prophet places the grave of Rachel north of Jerusalem in a place called Ramah (31:15).

Reuben, Israel's oldest son, has intercourse with Bihah, his father's concubine. This upsets Israel, and he will eventually curse Reuben, making him lose his position as the oldest son. Now that Jacob has twelve sons, the author can produce a list of the sons and their mothers. At this point, Jacob returns home to his father Isaac. Isaac died at the age of 180 years. His sons, Esau and Jacob, bury him.

Lectio Divina

Spend 8 to 10 minutes in silent contemplation of the following passage:

> The children of Abraham are increasing rapidly as God promised. In the New Testament, Jesus Christ, who is God, made another promise. He promised to be with us until the end of time and told us to multiply by spreading his word to all nations. God's promise is proven in the story of Abraham's family, and Christ's promise is continuing to be fulfilled throughout the world.

✠ *What can I learn from this passage?*

Edomite Lists (36)

The Priestly author provides a genealogy of Esau's family. The name Esau also refers to Edom. Esau took wives from among the Canaanite women, had a number of children, and moved to the land of Seir, away from his brother Jacob because their possessions became too great for them to live together. Esau is the ancestor of the Edomites. The author names the kings who reigned in the land of Edom before any kings reigned over the Israelites. This reference to the kings of Israel shows that the narrative and genealogy in this passage were composed after kings reigned in Israel.

Now that the author has named the offspring of Esau, he will disappear from the story.

Day 5: Joseph the Dreamer (37)

The Priestly author begins this chapter with a typical statement that this is the story of the family of Jacob. He links Jacob's settling in the land of Canaan with the land of his father's sojourn. In this Priestly account, Joseph appears at the age of seventeen tending the flocks with his brothers, Dan and Naphtali (the sons of Bilah, the handmaid of Rachel), and Gad and Asher (the sons of Zilpah, the handmaid of Leah). Although the author says that Joseph brought some type of bad report about them, he says no more about the bad report.

Jacob loves Joseph more than his brothers because, as the author mistakenly says, he was a child of his old age. Actually, when Joseph was born, Jacob was young and robust enough to keep working for Laban and raising his own flock (30:22–43). This discrepancy points to a different source for parts of the Joseph story. Actually, Jacob loved Joseph most because he was the child of Rachel, the wife he loved most. Jacob makes a long ornamental tunic for Joseph, which is a sign of great honor and which would naturally cause some jealousy among the brothers. The story does not tell us that it was a coat of many colors as found in the Greek and Latin versions of the Bible.

The story of Joseph presents its hero as one who receives messages in dreams and one who interprets the dreams of others. Joseph tells his brothers about a dream in which his sheaf stands in an upright position and their sheaves circle his and bow down before it. The brothers become more incensed with Joseph, mockingly asking if he is going to make himself a king over them. Joseph reveals another dream to his brothers in which the sun, moon, and eleven stars were bowing down to him. Even Jacob becomes incensed at this dream, asking if it means that Joseph's mother, father, and brothers are to bow down before him. The inclusion of Joseph's mother in Jacob's dream is further evidence that the portions of the story have come from another source different from Jacob's earlier adventures, since it speaks of Joseph's mother as still living.

In the Joseph stories, the author makes use of doublets, which present episodes in series of twos. Joseph has two dreams. The story does not follow the Eloist use of heavenly visitors coming in dreams, since Joseph does not have heavenly visitors, but dreams that he interprets. Although the brothers of Joseph and Jacob his father become irate over the dreams, they lived in an era when people took dreams seriously. The author tells us that Jacob kept the matter in mind, as though he had to mull over it.

One day, Jacob sends Joseph to determine if all was well with his brothers who were tending the flock at Shechem, which is about fifty miles from Hebron where Jacob was residing. When his brothers see him from a distance, they exclaim, "Here comes that dreamer" (37:19). They plot to kill him and throw him into a cistern, which was a large pit for gathering rainwater. It was useful as a prison from which no one could escape without help, and also as a place to hide the body of a dead victim.

Reuben, whom the Eloist author treats favorably in several passages, attempts to save Joseph by suggesting that they throw him into the cistern without killing him. His intent was to save Joseph later and bring him back to his father. It was believed at the time that when someone was killed, the blood on the ground would cry out and the murderer would be discovered. The brothers plot to take Joseph's robe, soak it in the blood of a goat, and bring the coat to their father with word that a wild animal killed Joseph.

After the brothers strip Joseph of his tunic and throw him into the cistern, a caravan of Ishmaelites come by, and Judah, not wishing to have the blood of their brother on his hands, suggests that they sell Joseph to the Ishmaelites. His brothers agree. This is actually one of two stories mingled together here. The story turns immediately to some Medianite traders who pull Joseph out of the cistern and sell him to the Ishmaelites for twenty pieces of silver.

The story returns to the previous Eloist story and Reuben comes to free Joseph, but he is not in the cistern. Reuben tears his garments as a sign of grief. The brothers dip Joseph's cloak in the blood of a goat and send someone to Jacob to ask if this is the tunic of his son, Joseph. Jacob recognizes the tunic and cries out in grief that Joseph has been torn to pieces by a wild animal. Jacob refuses to accept consolation from his sons and daughters and declared that he will go to Sheol, the land of the dead, grieving over his son. Sheol was considered a place of doom and gloom. In the meanwhile, the Medianites (not the Ishmaelites who supposedly bought Joseph from the Medianites) sell Joseph in Egypt to Potiphar, an official of Pharaoh and his chief steward.

Lectio Divina

Spend 8 to 10 minutes in silent contemplation of the following passage:

In the Gospel of Matthew, we read about another Joseph who is a dreamer, namely Joseph, the husband of Mary. In the infancy narrative, Joseph receives advice and warnings in dreams. The Joseph story in Genesis tells how the Israelites came into Egypt, while Joseph in the Gospel of Matthew receives word in a dream to take Mary as his wife, to flee to Egypt to avoid the killing of the innocents, and eventually to leave Egypt. The two Joseph stories tell us that God has a plan for creation, and we are part of the plan as long as we respond to the promptings of the Spirit in our lives.

✠ *What can I learn from this passage?*

Day 6: Judah and Tamar (38)

The story of Judah and Tamar interrupts the story of Joseph, although it does deal with Judah, one of the two brothers who wanted to avoid killing Joseph. Judah marries a Canaanite woman who bears sons named Er, Onan, and Shelah. Judah obtains a wife named Tamar for Er, but Er offends the Lord, and the Lord takes his life. According to the levirate law, when a man dies with no heirs, his brother is to have intercourse with his brother's wife, and all male heirs would be considered as belonging to the deceased brother. This would assure that the family line of the brother would continue.

With the death of Er, Judah gives Onan to Er's wife, Tamar, but Onan for some reason wastes his seed and does not produce an offspring for his brother's line. Since Onan offended the Lord, the Lord takes his life also. Judah's third boy, Shelah, is still young, so Judah returns Tamar to her father's house until Shelah is of age. Time passes, Shelah comes of age, but Judah makes no move to have Shelah fulfill the levirate law. Perhaps he feared that if Shelah died, he would have no male heirs to carry on his name.

One day, when Tamar hears that Judah is going to shear his sheep, she disguises herself as a prostitute and sits where Judah would have to pass her. By this time, Judah's wife had died. Judah, not recognizing Tamar and thinking she was a harlot, has intercourse with her and promises to send a goat from his flock as payment. She asks for his seal, cord, and staff as a pledge that he would send the goat. The seal hung around the neck with a cord and was used for making an image on clay tablets which was the sign of the owner. The staff would also identify its owner. Judah gives them to her.

When Judah sends a friend with a goat to redeem the seal, cord, and staff, no one could report knowing of any harlot in that area. Later, Judah learns that Tamar was pregnant, and he orders that she be burned. Although her husband had died, she was still considered to be betrothed to Er and therefore guilty of adultery. As she is being brought out to be burnt, she sends word to her father-in-law that she has become pregnant by the man who owns the seal, cord, and staff. Judah recognizes them and has to admit that she was right in what she did, since he did not give his third son to her.

When the time of her delivery arrives, she gives birth to twins. The manner of the birth is reminiscent of the birth of Jacob and Esau. The first puts out his hand and the midwife ties a crimson thread around it. When he withdraws his hand, his brother is born first. She names him Perez, which is a Hebrew word for "breach," and when his brother comes out with the crimson thread, she names him Zerah, a name linked with the Hebrew word for the red light of dawn, an apparent allusion to the crimson thread. Ironically, the line of Judah would continue through the offspring of Tamar. King David would be named as a descendant of Perez and not of Zerah. Tamar's name would find a place in the genealogy of Jesus.

Lectio Divina

Spend 8 to 10 minutes in silent contemplation of the following passage:

In the Gospel of John, the scribes and Pharisees bring a woman caught in adultery to Jesus to ask if they should stone her as Moses directed. Jesus' answer was that the one without sin should throw the first stone. Judah, in this story, was prepared to burn Tamar until she convinces him that he is not without sin.

✠ *What can I learn from this passage?*

Review Questions

1. What is significant about Jacob's dream of a stairway to heaven?
2. Why do you think God allowed men to have so many wives and concubines in the days of Abraham and Jacob?
3. Who was more deceptive, Jacob or Laban? Explain.

The Family of Israel Settles in Egypt

GENESIS 39—50

But Joseph replied to them (his brothers), "Do not fear. Can I take the place of God? Even though you meant harm to me, God meant it for good, to achieve this present end, the survival of many people" (50:19–20).

Opening Prayer (SEE PAGE 16)

Context

Part 1: Genesis 39—41 Joseph becomes a slave of an official of Pharaoh, but the official's wife accuses Joseph of attempting to seduce her and Joseph is thrown into prison. In prison, Joseph interprets the dreams of two others in prison with him, telling one he will find favor with Pharaoh and the other that he will be killed soon. Sometime later, Pharaoh has a dream, and when he hears about Joseph interpreting dreams, he sends for him. Joseph proceeds to tell Pharaoh that God is saying that there will be seven years of plenty followed by seven years of famine. Pharaoh places Joseph in charge of Egypt, second only to Pharaoh. There, Joseph has two sons. During the years of plenty, Joseph oversees the gathering of supplies to last during the seven years of famine.

Part 2: Genesis 42—50 Joseph's family needs supplies and makes a total of three trips to Egypt for supplies. They do not recognize

Joseph, who makes their visits painful and frightening. Joseph reveals himself to his brothers and tells them to bring their father, their households, and all their family into Egypt. Joseph and Pharaoh welcome them and give them some lush grazing ground. Jacob is overjoyed and proclaims that now that he has seen his son, he is ready to die. Jacob dies in Egypt and is brought in a grand manner to the tomb purchased by Abraham for his family. When Joseph dies, he makes the Israelites promise that when they depart the land of Egypt, they will take his bones with them.

PART 1: GROUP STUDY (GENESIS 39—41)

Read aloud Genesis 39—41.

39 Joseph's Temptation

The Ishmaelites sold Joseph to Potiphar, an Egyptian official of Pharaoh and his chief steward. When Potiphar saw that the Lord was with Joseph, he put Joseph in charge of his household. He trusted Joseph so thoroughly that he gave no thought to anything except the food he ate. The Yahwist author describes Joseph in a heroic manner as well-built and handsome. Unfortunately, his attractiveness led Potiphar's wife to tempt him, inviting him to lie with her. Joseph refused, unwilling to break his trust with his master and unwilling to sin against God.

One day, when the household servants were absent, Potiphar's wife tempts him again and grabs his cloak as he runs off. She cries out until her household staff arrives and she claims that Joseph tried to "amuse himself at my expense" (39:17) She produced his cloak as proof. When Joseph's master heard his wife's story, he had Joseph put in prison.

40 Dreams Interpreted

Joseph meets the royal cupbearer and baker who were imprisoned by Pharaoh. The chief steward assigns Joseph to them. Both had dreams that Joseph interprets for them. The cupbearer dreamed of a vine with three branches, blossoms, and clusters of ripened grapes that the cupbearer squeezed into the cup and put it in Pharaoh's hand. Joseph tells him that in three days he will be restored to his position as chief cupbearer. Joseph requests that the cupbearer remember him to Pharaoh, since he was kidnapped from the land of the Hebrews and is innocent of any crime. The image of the "land of the Hebrews" shows that the story was written at a later date, since at the time when Joseph lived, the land belonged to the Canaanites.

The chief baker says that in his dream, he had three breadbaskets on his head, and in the top one were all kinds of bakery products which the birds were eating from the baskets on his head. Joseph has dire news for the chief baker, telling him that in three days Pharaoh will impale him on a stake and the birds will be eating his flesh. Three days later, Pharaoh gives a banquet to all his servants, and he restores the chief cupbearer to his office and impales the chief baker. The chief cupbearer forgets about Joseph and his request.

41 Pharaoh's Dream

Two years after Joseph interpreted the dreams of the chief cupbearer and chief baker, Pharaoh has two dreams in which he sees seven fat and healthy cows come up out of the Nile with seven emaciated cows standing behind them. The gaunt cows devour the healthy, fat cows. In his second dream, he dreams of seven fat and healthy ears of grain growing on a single stalk. Behind them were seven thin and scorched ears of grain which swallowed up the fat ears.

The next morning ,Pharaoh had all the magicians and sages of Egypt called to interpret his dream, but they could not. Then, the chief cupbearer remembers Joseph and his interpretation of his dream and that of the chief baker. Pharaoh has Joseph brought from prison. Since he was following the Semitic traditions of allowing his beard to grow, he shaves as the Egyptians do.

Joseph proceeds to interpret the dreams for Pharaoh, telling him that God is telling Pharaoh that seven years of plenty are about to take place followed by seven years of famine. He urges Pharaoh to place someone in charge of organizing for storing up food in the first seven years and distributing it during the second seven years. Pharaoh puts Joseph in charge of the land of Egypt, second only to Pharaoh. He takes off his signet ring and gives it to Joseph as a sign of the authority he is bestowing on him.

He dresses him in robes of fine linen, puts a gold chain around his neck, and assigns him to ride in the second chariot after Pharaoh.

Pharaoh gives Joseph an Egyptian woman as his wife and Joseph sets about the task of collecting food for the first seven years. Before the famine struck, Joseph becomes the father of two sons. He names his firstborn Manasseh because God made him forgetful of his troubles, which is the meaning of the name, and the second he names Ephraim because God made him fruitful in the land of his affliction, which is the meaning of the name. When the famine struck throughout the land, there was food in Egypt. The author states that the whole world came to Egypt to buy grain.

The use of doublets continues in these stories as the two men, chief cupbearer and chief baker, are imprisoned. Pharaoh has two dreams. In the first dream are two types of cows, healthy and gaunt, and two types of grain, healthy and shriveled. There are also two sets of seven years, one set full of plenty and a second set plagued with famine.

Review Questions

1. Do you believe that the story of Joseph's imprisonment shows us that God can draw good out of evil?
2. What comparisons can you find between Joseph the son of Jacob and Joseph the husband of Mary?
3. Why do you think Joseph is placed in a high position in Egypt?

Closing Prayer (SEE PAGE 16)

Pray the closing prayer now or after *lectio divina*.

Lectio Divina (SEE PAGE 9)

Relax your body and maintain a posture of prayer (back straight, eyes shut, feet flat on the floor). This exercise can take as long as you want, but in the context of this Bible study, 10 to 20 minutes should be sufficient.

The meditations that follow are provided only to help group participants use this prayer form, but note that *lectio* is intended to bring one to a place of prayerful contemplation where the Word of God speaks to the hearer from his or her heart. (See page 9 for further instruction.)

Joseph's Temptation (39)

The story of Joseph's temptation recalls the words of the Lord's Prayer where we pray "lead us not into temptation." Avoiding temptation is difficult, but when a person who is innocent is falsely accused and punished, another temptation to anger and resentment arise. There is no evidence that Joseph the dreamer allowed another temptation to grip him. A virtuous person who overcomes temptation can be tempted by pride. There seems to be no relief from temptations, which is why we need to pray not to be led into them.

✠ *What can I learn from this passage?*

Dreams Interpreted (40)

Joseph interprets a dream for the chief cupbearer and asks that he remember him to Pharaoh, but he forgets about Joseph. Good deeds are often overlooked or forgotten about. In Luke's Gospel, Jesus heals ten lepers and only one returns glorifying God. Jesus sadly asks, "Where are the other nine" (17:17)? Even God appreciates our gratitude for the gifts we receive.

✠ *What can I learn from this passage?*

Pharaoh's Dream (41)

Pharaoh has dreams, and Joseph is able to change them into hopes for the future. Pharaoh can now dream of having food for his people during the time of the famine. When Joseph was living with Jacob, he may have had dreams of continuing to live life as a shepherd, but his dreams changed because of his ability to interpret dreams that came during sleep. Our faith tells us that God has a dream for our life, namely our salvation and our particular call in life. God fills us with dreams and hopes for the future so that God's plan for creation can move forward.

✠ *What can I learn from this passage?*

PART 2: INDIVIDUAL STUDY (GENESIS 42—50)

Day 1: Joseph's Brothers in Egypt (42—43)

Jacob sends ten of his sons to Egypt to buy food. Jacob does not send Benjamin, since he could not bear the loss of the only surviving son of his favorite wife, Rachel. Joseph recognizes his brothers, but they do not recognize him, since he most likely shaved his beard according to Egyptian customs. He would also be wearing Egyptian clothing and speaking the Egyptian language, making him appear to need an interpreter to speak with his brothers. When the brothers come into Joseph's presence, they bow down to him. Joseph recalls his dream when he told his brothers that their sheaves bowed down before his sheave.

Joseph accuses them of being spies, seeking some revenge for their actions against him. Accusing them of spying would not be out of the ordinary, since the Egyptians would have to worry about spies looking for a weakness in the country's security. Other nations, knowing that Egypt had stored up an abundance of food, would want to plunder Egypt and take the food for themselves. The brothers plead their innocence and explain that they are twelve brothers, one of whom is no more. Significantly, they do not say that he is dead. Joseph tells them that they are to remain in jail while one of them goes to get the youngest child. He puts them in jail for three days, perhaps to make them ponder the danger they are in. After three days, he relents and allows nine of the brothers to return home. He binds up Simeon in their sight and keeps him a prisoner.

Reuben, who is treated well by the Eloist author, reminds his brothers that he told them to do no wrong to the boy, and he complains that they refused to listen to him. He tells them that they are now paying the price for his blood. The brothers did not know that Joseph understood what was being said. Joseph turns his back on them and weeps. He then sent orders that the containers of his brothers were to be filled with grain and their money placed in each one's sack. They were also to receive provisions for their journey. When the brothers camped for the night, they discover the money and become frightened. They wonder whether they would be accused of stealing when they returned.

When they arrive home and tell their father, Jacob, about their visit and the command that they return with Benjamin to prove that they are not spies. Jacob stands firm, saying that Joseph is no more and adding that Simeon is no more, apparently believing that Simeon will never be released or that he is dead. Reuben again takes the heroic stance when he tells Jacob that he may kill his two sons if he does not return with Benjamin. Jacob refuses to allow Benjamin to leave him, fearing that some disaster will visit him on the journey, and that he, Jacob, will go down to Sheol in deep grief.

After the grain they bought from Joseph ran out, Jacob told his sons to return to Egypt for more food. Judah, who is treated well by the Yahwist writer of this episode, states that they will not go unless Benjamin goes with them. Jacob asks why they had to tell the man (Joseph) that they had a brother, and Judah says that the man kept asking about the health of the father and whether they had another brother. Actually, the brothers volunteered the information without being asked for it. Judah promises to protect Benjamin or suffer forever, bearing the disgrace and blame. His frustration with his father shows when he declares that they could have been there and back by now.

Finally, Jacob agrees to allow Benjamin to go, and he provides double the amount of money needed to pay for the new supplies along with those they bought on their first visit. He also adds gifts for the man, whom none of them have recognized as Joseph. Until this point, no one mentions Simeon, but Jacob prays that God Almighty will grant them mercy and allow the other brother and Benjamin to go.

When the brothers arrive in Egypt with their brother Benjamin, Joseph orders that an animal be slaughtered and prepared for them to dine with him. When the brothers see that they are being led to Joseph's house, they become concerned, thinking that they would be attacked and taken as slaves. Joseph's steward assures them that he has received the money they brought with them, and that all is well. He then leads Simeon to them. The steward brings them into the house, gives them water to wash their feet, and feeds their donkeys.

The brothers set their gifts out for Joseph, whom, they hear, would dine with them. Joseph asks about the sons' father and asks if Benjamin was the young brother about whom they spoke earlier. When Joseph sees Benjamin, he leaves the room and weeps. Later at mealtime, Joseph eats apart from everyone, perhaps due to his exalted position. The Jews eat at a different table than the Egyptians, which was the custom in that day. Joseph sends portions from his table to the brothers as a sign of friendship and acceptance. Benjamin, Joseph's brother, receives five times more than the rest. They drink and enjoy the occasion.

Lectio Divina

Spend 8 to 10 minutes in silent contemplation of the following passage:

The Gospel of Mark tells the story of a blind man whom Jesus heals. Instead of the blind man seeing instantly, he recovers his sight slowly. He first sees people looking like trees and walking, but when Jesus touches him a second time, he sees clearly (see Mark 8:22–26). The symbol of the healing in the gospel story is that Jesus' disciples, although they realize that there is something special about Jesus, do not yet clearly understand Jesus. Understanding will come gradually.

Each time Joseph tests his brothers, he is pressuring them into realizing the full impact of their sin in selling Joseph into slavery. When we sin, we must take time to ponder the meaning of Jesus' life, love, and message and recognize the impact of our sins on God's love for us. The closer we draw to Christ, the more we regret any time when we have ignored or rejected him through sin.

✠ *What can I learn from this passage?*

Day 2: The Final Test and Truth (44—45)

Joseph has his steward fill the bags of Jacob's sons with as much food as they could carry, but he also has the steward put his silver goblet in the bag of the youngest. The silver goblet was a sacred vessel into which some liquid would be poured and some predictions could be made. Although the Israelites frowned upon divination, it seems that God allows Joseph to follow some Egyptian practices. When they leave and are far out of the city, Joseph sends his steward after them and accuses them of stealing the goblet. The brothers are so sure of their innocence that they vow that if anyone of them has taken the goblet, he shall die and the rest shall become Joseph's slaves. The steward appears generous in refusing their suggestion and declares that only the one who stole the goblet would become the master's slave. All the brothers willingly lower their bags to the ground, and to their horror, the goblet is found in Benjamin's bag. They all return to the city.

The Yahwist author again makes Judah the center of his story. He notes that when Judah and his brothers enter Joseph's house, Joseph asks how they could do such a thing. He claims that they should have known that he would know what happened by divination. Judah speaks on behalf of the group, noting their guilt and offering all of the brothers as slaves, not just the one in possession of the goblet. The guilt expressed by Judah could not only refer to the goblet, but to recognition of what they had done to their brother, Joseph. Joseph appears to act magnanimously in saying that everyone may go free except the one in whose possession the goblet was found. The author has already revealed Joseph's ploy in deceiving the brothers. He has no intention of making any of them slaves. At this point, however, Joseph declares that Benjamin shall become his slave.

Judah expresses recognition that Joseph is equal to Pharaoh, a form of praise given before one makes a plea. He tells of their encounter with Jacob and how the loss of Benjamin would kill his father. Judah tells how he promised his father that he would bring the boy back or suffer the blame forever, and begs Joseph to take him as a slave in the place of Benjamin.

Joseph could no longer restrain himself in front of his attendants, so he sends them out and reveals himself to his brothers. He cries with such intensity that the Egyptians hear him and news reaches Pharaoh. Joseph says to his brothers, "I am Joseph," and he immediately asks about the health of his father. When his astonished brothers could not respond, he removes from them the blame for selling him to Egypt by saying that it was God who sent him to Egypt to save a remnant of Israel. God made him a father to Pharaoh and gave him this great power in Egypt. He then urges his brothers to hurry home and to return back with their families and all they own to settle in an area he names as Goshen. He promises to care for them and directs them to tell his father about his high position in Egypt.

Joseph embraces Benjamin and kisses all of his brothers. Only then were his speechless brothers able to converse with him.

When Pharaoh learns that Joseph's brothers had come, Pharaoh is pleased. He orders Joseph to have his brothers tell all their family, their children, their wives, and their father, to load up their wagons and come to Egypt where they will live off the fat of the land. They are not to be concerned about their belongings, for the best of Egypt will be theirs.

Joseph gives them wagons as Pharaoh had ordered, along with provisions for the journey with a special gift of money to Benjamin and five sets of clothing. He sends to his father the best of all that Egypt had to offer and tells his brothers not to quarrel on the way. When the brothers report to Jacob all that had happened and that Joseph is alive, he does not believe them, but when he sees the gifts, his spirit comes to life. He accepts their word that Joseph is alive and declares that he must go and see him before he dies.

Lectio Divina

Spend 8 to 10 minutes in silent contemplation of the following passage:

> In the Gospel of Matthew, Jesus says, "Come to me, all you who labor and are burdened, and I will give you rest." After all the hardships endured by Jacob and after the frightening tests given to the brothers, Joseph calls them to come for rest from their worries. He is like Christ. He is the son chosen by God to bring salvation to Israel, just as Jesus offers the hope of rest and salvation to those who are willing to endure all for the love of Christ.

✠ *What can I learn from this passage?*

Day 3: Israel in Egypt (46—47:26)

The Eloist author presents a different reason for Jacob making the decision to migrate with his family to Egypt. In a nighttime vision, Jacob hears God's call and answers "Here I am," a sign of willingness to respond to God. In the vision, God is revealed as the God of his father, and God tells Jacob not to be afraid of going to Egypt. God promises that in Egypt the descendants of Jacob will become a great nation. At this juncture, God pledges to go down to Egypt with him and to bring him back after his son

Joseph has closed Jacob's eyes, that is, to bring him back to the land of Canaan after he dies. Jacob's whole family, along with their livestock and possessions, go to Egypt.

There is a short interruption by the Priestly author who adds another genealogy to the epic. He lists Jacob's sons and their offspring. The author lists seventy people, which is the traditional number of those who settled in Egypt. The genealogy is clearly structured by the author to teach a message and should not be taken as a historically accurate list.

Judah goes out to prepare a meeting between Joseph and Jacob at Goshen. When Joseph sees his father, he weeps. Jacob proclaims that now he can die, since he saw that his son Joseph is truly alive. Joseph describes his plans of meeting with Pharaoh to inform him that his family is a family of shepherds who brought their flocks and herds with them. He instructs his family that when they come before Pharaoh, they are to tell him that they are shepherds. In doing this, Joseph is able to assure that they are able to remain at Goshen where there is land for grazing. It also separates the Israelite shepherds from the Egyptians who abhor shepherds.

Joseph chooses five of his brothers to appear before Pharaoh. They inform Pharaoh that they were shepherds and explain that the famine drove them to this land. The esteem of Pharaoh for Joseph proves itself in the generous present of land made by Pharaoh and the prestigious honor of caring for Pharaoh's livestock.

Jacob's appearance before Pharaoh is congenial and simple. When Pharaoh asks Jacob how old he is, Jacob answers that he is 130 years old. He notes that this is far fewer than Abraham, who lived to an age of 175, and Isaac, who lived to the age of 180. The ages may not be actual and may be the result of stories passing from generation to the next before they were committed to writing. The family settled in the lush land of Goshen and Joseph provided for all the needs of Jacob's whole household.

Joseph continues to sell food to the Egyptians during the famine, but the people soon run out of money and give their livestock and their lives in exchange for food. Joseph gives them seed for planting and orders that a fifth of the produce shall go to the Pharaoh. The only ones exempt from the famine and slavery were the priests who received an allowance from the government and who did not have to spend their money for food.

Lectio Divina

Spend 8 to 10 minutes in silent contemplation of the following passage:

> The people of Jesus' day knew that the blessings given to the family of Israel by God would cease in the centuries ahead and that the people would be living in slavery instead of living off the fat of the land. Thankfully though, the people kept their faith through the period of plenty and their final period of servitude. In Luke's Gospel, Jesus tells a story of a rich fool who planned to build larger barns so that he could retire and live in luxury, but God calls him a fool, because that night God would take his life (see 12:16–21). Jesus tells this story to remind us that our true treasure in life is remaining faithful to God in good times and in bad, as the Israelites did.

✠ *What can I learn from this passage?*

Day 4: Jacob's Blessing and Testament (47:27—49:27)

Jacob lives in Egypt for seventeen years, during which time his family prospers. At this time, Jacob makes Joseph put his hand under his thigh and swear that he would bury his father at the family gravesite, which was in the land of Canaan and was the place where Abraham and Isaac were buried.

Upon learning of his father's impending death, Joseph takes his two sons, Ephraim and Manasseh, with him to be with Jacob. Jacob adopts Joseph's two sons as his own by taking them on his knees and giving them the rights belonging to the other sons. The story becomes confusing, since it was reported that Jacob spent seventeen years in Egypt, yet he is here asking Joseph who these two boys are. The confusion comes from the fact that an editor is joining two traditions together here to explain some later historical events. In this passage, Joseph explains to Jacob that through the goodness of God, two sons were born to him in Egypt.

Jacob was old and his eyes were dim. Joseph places the older son, Manasseh, on Jacob's right so that he will receive the greater blessing, and Ephraim, the second son, on the left. Jacob crosses his hands so that his right hand, the hand of honor, is on Ephraim and his left on Manasseh.

When Joseph sees his father place his right hand on Ephraim, he tries to remove the hand from Ephraim to Manasseh, since Manasseh was the firstborn. Jacob declares that he is aware of what he is doing and states that the older boy would be the father of a great people, but that Ephraim would surpass him. The story follows other stories in Genesis where the second son was chosen over the first. Abel supplanted Cain (chapter 4), Isaac supplanted Ishmael (17:19–21), Jacob supplanted Esau (chapter 27), and Perez supplanted Zerah (38:27–30). God chooses as God wills.

Jacob blesses the boys in the name of the God of Abraham and Isaac, the God who was his shepherd, and the angel who delivered him from all harm. This is the one and same God at different eras in the history of the patriarchs. The angel who delivered Jacob from all harm is also God. Jacob passes the promise of descendants that came to Abraham and Isaac onto the boys, praying that they may have a large number of descendants.

Jacob's last words to Joseph tell him that God will be with him and restore him to the land of his ancestors. This could refer to Joseph's burial there and also to the return of his offspring to the Promised Land. He honors Joseph as the one above his brothers and gives him Shechem that he captured from the Amorites with his sword and bow. According to chapter 34, Jacob did not take Shechem.

Jacob predicts what will happen in days to come for his offspring. In reality, the blessings refer to a later time in history, and they seem to come from several different authors, pointing not always to the sons but to the tribes who gained their names from them. An editor brought them together.

Jacob speaks first of Reuben, the oldest of the sons. He excels in rank and power, but he will no longer excel because he slept with his father's concubine. Jacob speaks harshly of Simeon and Levi because of their violent response to the rape of Dinah, and he curses them for their cruelty at Shecham and predicts their demise. Judah receives praise from Jacob. He is the powerful warrior, the one who will triumph over all the brothers. The scepter, which apparently refers to authority, shall not leave him and his people will follow his authority. The Davidic line will come from that of Judah. Zebulun shall settle by the sea and be a haven for ships. Issachar found security in servile labor as a slave. Dan shall be a judge and be like a snake at the roadside, one that is shrewd enough to destroy evil. Gad will be attacked by raiders but will overcome. Asher's tribe shall live in a fertile and rich area which produces abundantly. Nephtali shall prosper.

The longest section concerns Joseph. Joseph lives with abundance and, although attacked often, he remains a conqueror with the help of the God of Jacob and the Rock of Israel, namely God. An abundance of blessings from God will accompany Joseph. Benjamin is a successful warrior tribe.

Lectio Divina

Spend 8 to 10 minutes in silent contemplation of the following passage:

> The choice of the second-born son in the stories of Genesis shows us that God chooses as God wills. When we read the Acts of the Apostles, we discover that it was the missionary efforts and letters of Paul that had the greatest effect on the future of the Church. Paul, a later apostle who did not travel with Jesus during his public life, was the one chosen to teach us how to live as Church. He introduced us to the image of the Church as the Body of Christ and the reality that we all receive a particular call in God's plan for the Church on earth. God chooses as God wills.

✠ *What can I learn from this passage?*

Day 5: Death and Funeral of Jacob (49:28—50)

Jacob blesses his sons and instructs them as he did Joseph that he is to be buried at the same site as Abraham and Sarah, Isaac and Rebekah, and Leah. Jacob dies.

Joseph weeps bitterly when Jacob dies, and he orders the physicians to embalm his father. The embalming takes forty days, and the Egyptians mourn Jacob for seventy days. Joseph receives permission to carry out his oath about the burial commands of his father. A procession of dignitaries, Joseph's whole household, and many others proceeded to the land of Canaan for the burial of Jacob. According to this tradition, he was buried with his ancestors as he requested. Jacob's family returns to Egypt after the burial.

Upon the death of Jacob, Joseph's brothers fear that he will retaliate for the way they treated him when he was with them tending the flocks. They report to him that Jacob told them to go to Joseph and ask that he forgive the wrongdoings of his brothers. When Joseph weeps, his brothers weep with him and offer themselves as his slaves. Joseph calmed them, saying, "Can I take the place of God?" Joseph believes that God has forgiven them. Since this is so, how could he not forgive them? Although they meant to punish him, God was at work and destined the betrayal to achieve the survival of many people. Joseph promises to provide for them and their children.

God blesses Joseph by allowing him to see Ephraim's children to the third generation and the children of Manasseh's son, Machir, who was born on his knee, meaning that Joseph adopted him.

When Joseph was dying, he predicts that God would lead the Israelites from Egypt to the land God promised on oath to Abraham, Isaac, and Jacob. He makes those present swear that when God takes care of them, they must bring his bones with them. This is a reference to the day when the Israelites leave Egypt. He dies at the age of 110, and, after being embalmed, was laid in a coffin in Egypt.

Lectio Divina

Spend 8 to 10 minutes in silent contemplation of the following passage:

The people of Joseph's day believed that one's mortality continued through their male heirs, which is why having a male child was important to the people. They believed that the spirit of Abraham, Isaac, and Jacob somehow continued in their offspring. Today, we believe that the chosen leaders of Israel are saints sharing in God's glory. In the gospels, we read of the resurrection of Jesus, and we learn that we too will rise in Christ. We believe that the patriarchs, Jesus, and all of us will share together in God's glory.

✠ *What can I learn from this passage?*

Review Questions

1. What does Joseph's testing of his brothers tell us about Joseph?
2. What does Joseph's forgiveness of his brothers tell us about him?
3. What is the significance of Jacob choosing Joseph's second son over his first son?

LESSON 6

The Book of Exodus

Exodus From Egypt

EXODUS 1—7:7

"This is what you will tell the Israelites: I AM has sent me to you." God spoke further to Moses: "This is what you will say to the Israelites: The LORD, the God of your ancestors, the God of Abraham, the God of Isaac, and the God of Jacob, has sent me to you" (3:14–15).

Opening Prayer (SEE PAGE 16)

Context

Part 1: Exodus 1—3:15 Four hundred years elapse between the end of Genesis and the beginning of the Book of Exodus. The title of the book, which means "departure," comes from the Septuagint, a Greek translation of the Bible produced about 150 years before Christ. The Hebrew name for the book was Shemoth, which means "Names," and it comes from the opening phrase in the book, "These are the names..."(1:1). Pharaoh commands the midwives to kill the Israelite male children when they are born; but instead, the midwives let them live. When the child who will eventually bear the name Moses is hidden among the reeds in the Nile, Pharaoh's daughter finds him. She unknowingly chooses Moses' mother to nurse him. When Moses kills an Egyptian, he flees to the desert where he settles down, marries, and has a child. God visits Moses in the desert and commissions him to lead the Israelites out of slavery.

Part 2: Exodus 3:16—7:7 Moses meets with the elders and tells them that the God of their ancestors has sent him to free the people. God predicted that the king would refuse to allow the Israelites to leave. The Lord will send maladies upon the Egyptians to the point that the Egyptians will want them to leave. The Israelites will take silver, gold articles, and clothing with them from the Egyptians. The Lord appoints Aaron to be Moses' spokesperson. When Moses and Aaron ask Pharaoh to allow the people to leave and worship in the wilderness, Pharaoh retaliates by making life more miserable for the Israelites. God promises to fulfill the promise made in the past to Abraham, Isaac, and Israel.

PART 1: GROUP STUDY (EXODUS 1—3:15)

Read aloud Exodus 1—3:15.

1 Jacob's Descendants in Egypt

The author begins with the names of Jacob's sons and lists them according to their mothers. The first six are sons from Leah; Benjamin is Rachel's second son; Bilah, Rachel's handmaid, has two; and Zilpah, Leah's handmaid, has two. Joseph, her firstborn, is not added since he was already in Egypt when the family arrived there. Following the Priestly tradition, the author adds that the total number of Jacob's "direct" descendants was seventy.

The current Pharaoh, "who knew nothing of Joseph" (1:8), could mean that he had no knowledge about Joseph's place in Egypt's history, or that he cared little about the stories he heard about Joseph. He uses the Israelite slaves to build the cities of Pithon and Raamses, which are presumed to be in Goshen, although their actual locations are unknown. Despite the oppression, the Israelites continue to multiply and spread. Exodus states that rapid growth of the Israelites caused the Egyptians to loath them.

The king directs the midwives of the Hebrews to kill all the boys born to the Israelites and to spare the girls. The author names two midwives, Shiprah and Puah, who are most likely Egyptians, and they fear God so they did not kill the male children. They tell Pharaoh that the Hebrew women were so strong they give birth before the midwives arrived. God blesses the midwives, rewarding them with families. Pharaoh then orders his people to throw every newborn boy of the Israelites into the Nile but to allow the girls to live.

2:1–10 The Adoption of Moses

A child who would later be known as Moses is born into a family who were descendants of Levi, the third son of Jacob. After the birth of Moses, his mother places him in a basket and sets the basket among the reeds on the bank of the Nile. Later in Exodus, we will learn that the names of the child's parents are Amram and Jochebed, who also bore Aaron and Mariam (6:20). Mariam, the sister of the child, posts herself where she can secretly discover what happens to him.

There are parallels to the creation story in the birth of Moses. When he is born, his mother saw that he was a fine child, which means she saw that he was good, just as God saw that creation was good in the first creation story. The Hebrew word for the basket used to transport the child was the same word used for Noah's ark in the story of the Flood. Just as Noah was saved in the ark, so the child was saved in the basket. There is also a link with a future event. Just as the mother of the child places him among the reeds, the later story of Moses and the Israelites escaping from Egypt takes place as they pass through the Sea of Reeds, sometimes referred to as the Red Sea. In the story of Noah and the ark, Noah helped his family escape from people enslaved in a sin-filled world, so Moses will bring the Hebrew people to a new creation by helping them escape from the slavery of Egypt.

The author of the childhood of Moses wrote his narrative long after the event described and therefore places a series of ironic facts into the story. Pharaoh ordered that all the male newborn children be cast into the Nile. In one sense, the mother of the child follows Pharaoh's command by placing him in the Nile, but it is done with the help of a waterproof basket. The daughter of Pharaoh discovers the basket and takes pity on the child. Moses' sister asks Pharaoh's daughter if she wants her to find a Hebrew woman to nurse the child. When Pharaoh's daughter agrees, the child's sister brings the mother of the child to Pharaoh's daughter, and the daughter of Pharaoh offers the child's mother a wage for nursing him.

When the child grew to the age of two or three, the child's mother brings him to Pharaoh's daughter. Pharaoh's daughter takes the child as her son and names him Moses. The name may have referred to an Egyptian god of the Nile, but the author of the narrative may not be able to recall the source of the name and adapts the name to a Hebrew play on words that means, "I drew him out of the water." This could have a double meaning for the narrator of the story. Moses was drawn out of the water by Pharaoh's daughter, but he would also draw the Hebrews out of Egypt through the waters of the Red Sea.

2:11–22 Moses Flees to Midian

The author tells us that Moses grows up and witnesses the forced labor of his kinsmen. Moses encounters an Egyptian striking a Hebrew slave and, seeing no one, he kills the Egyptian and hides him in the sand. The next day, he comes across two Hebrews in a brawl and asks the one responsible for the encounter why he is striking his companion. The man asks Moses if he is thinking of killing him as he killed the Egyptian. When Pharaoh heard of this incident, he seeks to kill Moses who flees to the land of Midian. The land of Midian was the land settled by the descendants of Midian, who was a son of Abraham by Keturah (see Genesis 25:1–2).

Moses sits down by a well just as seven daughters of the priest of Midian come to draw water and to fill their troughs in order to water their father's flock. When shepherds come and drive them away, Moses successfully defends them and waters their flock. Then the daughters return home to their father Reuel and tell him about Moses, who orders them to invite Moses to have something to eat. The daughters describe Moses as an Egyptian, most likely due to his dress and familiarity with Egyptian language. Moses stays with them and eventually marries Zipporah, the daughter of Reuel. In the next chapter, we discover that Moses' father-in-law is identified as Jethro. Reuel was actually the grandfather of Zipporah. She bore a son to Moses named Gershom, which means that Moses was a stranger living in a foreign land.

2:23—3:15 The Burning Bush

After a period of time, the king of Egypt dies and is replaced by a new king who apparently knows of no reason to kill Moses. The new king makes no move to relieve the forced labor conditions of the Hebrews who cry out to God for help. God—heedful of the covenant made with Abraham, Isaac, and Jacob—witnesses the suffering of the Israelites. The passage from chapter 2:23 to 2:25 comes from the Priestly author and serves as a transition to God's visitation to Moses.

Moses has settled in Midian and is tending his father-in-law's flock. As one who must move with the flock for better pastures, Moses leads the flock to the mountain of God, known as Horeb. In the E source, the mountain is known as Horeb, but in the J and P source, it is known as Sinai. There is some question whether the names refer to the same mountain. Naming it as the "mountain of God" may indicate that it is a Midianite sacred mountain, or it may be in anticipation of God's later visitation to Moses on Mount Sinai.

On Mount Horeb, an angel of the Lord appears to Moses as fire flaming forth from a bush. The image of an angel of the Lord may refer to a messenger sent by God, or it may refer to a presence of God as it does in this passage: "Despite the flames, the bush is not consumed." God calls out to him from the bush, addressing Moses by name, and directs him to remove his shoes, since he is on sacred ground. The Lord says, "I am the God of your father...the God of Abraham, the God of Isaac, and the God of Jacob" (3:6). This greeting links Moses' vision with the covenants made to Abraham, Isaac, and Jacob. Since it was believed by the people of Moses' day that looking upon the Lord would be such an awesome experience that a person would die or cease to exist, Moses attempts to hide his face out of fear of looking upon God.

The Lord has heard the cry of the suffering Israelites and will lead them from the slavery of Egypt to a land flowing with milk and honey. The expression concerning the land flowing with milk and honey appears to be a proverb used to express the idea of a land of abundance. It refers to the country of the Canaanites, which includes a number of different tribes of people. Hearing the cry of the people, the Lord commissions Moses to go to Pharaoh to lead God's people out of Egypt.

Moses offers the first of four objections when he asks, "Who am I that I should go to Pharaoh and bring the Israelites out of Egypt" (3:11)? When the expression, "Who am I," is used, it is not a rejection, but a type of humble plea that is used by a subordinate when speaking to a superior. God promises to be with Moses; and the burning bush and God's vision will be a sign for Moses that he is sent by God. Moses will lead the people out from Egypt and worship the Lord on Mount Horeb.

Moses poses his second objection, asking what he shall respond if they ask him the name of the God of their ancestors. The Hebrew people have been in Egypt for a long period of time and some have begun to worship Egyptian gods, so Moses wants to identify the God who is sending him. God replies with the words, "I am who I am," "I AM," or Yahweh. The author introduces "Yahweh" here as though we are hearing it for the first time, although it was used in the Yahwist tradition beginning in Genesis where the author tells us that the people began to invoke the Lord by name (4:26).

Review Questions

1. Why doesn't Pharaoh care about the deeds of Joseph?
2. What does the childhood of Moses tell us about the providence of God?
3. Why is it significant that Moses learns the name of God?

Closing Prayer (SEE PAGE 16)

Pray the closing prayer now or after *lectio divina*.

Lectio Divina (SEE PAGE 9)

Relax your body and maintain a posture of prayer (back straight, eyes shut, feet flat on the floor). This exercise can take as long as you want, but in the context of this Bible study, 10 to 20 minutes should be sufficient.

The meditations that follow are provided only to help group participants use this prayer form, but note that *lectio* is intended to bring one to a place of prayerful contemplation where the Word of God speaks to the hearer from his or her heart. (See page 9 for further instruction.)

Jacob's Descendants in Egypt (1)

When Jesus is born, Joseph and Mary must take him to Egypt to avoid the killing of the innocents, a command issued by Herod the king when he heard that a newborn king was to be born in Bethlehem. The story parallels the story of the child Moses, who is saved by the daughter of Pharaoh of Egypt. In both cases, God protects the children, both of whom have a destiny in salvation. Moses was to save his people from the slavery of Egypt and Jesus would bring salvation for all people. In the case of both Moses and Jesus, accepting salvation depends on the free will of the people.

✠ *What can I learn from this passage?*

The Adoption of Moses (2:1–10)

There is an old maxim that says, "If you want to make God laugh, tell God your plans." The idea behind this adage is that many people make plans and begin to work toward a certain goal only to find themselves many years later in a life situation that is far from their original plans. One reality of life is that we not only work toward a certain goal, but time and life situations shape and even change us.

When Moses was being raised in the home of Pharaoh, no one realized that his familiarity with life within Pharaoh's court would enable him to deal more directly with the Egyptian leaders. When God found Moses in the wilderness tending his sheep, Moses was most likely content with his new form of life, but God laughed and chose Moses to endure the painful task of leading God's people to the chosen land. Many people can look at their life now and realize that this was not what they planned many decades earlier.

✠ *What can I learn from this passage?*

Moses Flees to Midian (2:11–22)

Just as Joseph had to flee from Bethlehem with Jesus, now Moses flees from Egypt. The parallel continues, showing how the interference of rulers such as Pharaoh and King Herod influence the events of their history. God is a God of history, which means for us that God deals with us in our historical and personal situation. In prayer, we speak to God about our needs and the needs of our world. The God of history touches our lives and those in the world around us.

✠ *What can I learn from this passage?*

The Burning Bush (2:23—3:15)

God comes to Moses in the form of a burning bush and shows God's concern for the people of Israel. In the gospels we learn of God's continual love for all people when we read, "God so loved the world that he gave his only Son, so that everyone who believes in him might not perish but might have eternal life" (John 3:16). In both cases, God takes the initiative and comes to bring salvation.

✠ *What can I learn from this passage?*

PART 2: INDIVIDUAL STUDY (EXODUS 3:16—7:7)

Day 1: God Directs Moses' Mission (3:16—4:9)

Moses and the elders are to go to the king of Egypt and report that the God of the Hebrews has come to meet them and that the king is to let them go for a three-day journey in the wilderness to offer sacrifice to the Lord. The Lord predicts that the king will not allow them to go, so God promises to strike the Egyptians with afflictions that will leave the people so anxious to see them go that they will not go empty-handed.

Moses continues his objections to the Lord, saying that the elders may not believe that the Lord did not appear to him. The Lord provides three signs that Moses may use to persuade them. The Lord has Moses throw his staff to the ground, and when he does, it becomes a snake. Then, the Lord bids Moses to grab the snake by the tail, and when Moses does so, it becomes a staff again. After this, the Lord asks Moses to put his hand in his cloak and take it out. When Moses pulls his hand out, his hand is covered with scales as white as snowflakes. So Moses repeats the action, pulling his hand out from his cloak once more and it is normal again. The Lord bids Moses to take some water from the Nile and pour it on the dry land where it will become blood. Each time the Egyptians disbelieve the sign, Moses is to turn to the next sign until all three have been used.

Lectio Divina

Spend 8 to 10 minutes in silent contemplation of the following passage:

The Lord prepares Moses for his visit to Pharaoh by giving him some miraculous signs as proof that God is with him. Moses will soon learn that no matter how many miraculous works a person performs, the people must be open to accepting the miracles. Jesus performed many miraculous deeds in his life, and many refused to accept him. Our acceptance of Christ's presence and blessings depends on our openness to Christ's presence in our life.

✠ *What can I learn from this passage?*

Day 2: Aaron to Speak for Moses (4:10–31)

Moses objects for the fourth time, saying that he lacks the gift of eloquence. He declares that he is "slow of speech and tongue" (4:10), which may point to some speech impediment or a lack of confidence in his ability to speak before groups. When God promises to help Moses speak, Moses remains adamant and begs God to send someone else. The Lord becomes angry with Moses, a statement that portrays God in a human manner.

God tells Moses that Aaron, his Levite brother, who is a good speaker, will soon arrive and rejoice when he sees Moses. God declares that the relationship between Moses and Aaron will be like the one between God and Moses. God puts words into the mouth of the prophets, and Moses, like God, will put words into Aaron's mouth. When God tells Moses to "take this staff" (4:17), it is not clear whether it is the staff that Moses previously threw to the ground or a new staff that God is giving to him.

Since those who sought Moses' life are dead, God directs Moses to return to Egypt. Although the author previously spoke of only one son for Moses, he writes that Moses takes his wife and his sons on his journey. The Lord God will harden the heart of Pharaoh, and he will not let the people go. Therefore, the Lord tells Moses to tell Pharaoh that he must let Israel leave Egypt so that they may serve the Lord. In this passage, the Lord refers to Israel as "my firstborn" (4:23) and predicts that the Lord will kill Pharaoh's firstborn since he refused to let God's people go.

On the journey, the Lord surprisingly intends to kill Moses. Zipporah, Moses' wife, acts quickly by taking a piece of flint and cutting off her sons' foreskin. The text says that she touched his feet, which is a euphemism used several times in the Scriptures to refer to genitals. The Lord apparently intended to kill Moses because Moses had not followed the covenant agreement between God and Abraham that called for the circumcision of all males. And it was Zipporah's action that led God to spare Moses.

God sends Aaron out to meet Moses on the mountain of God, and he kisses Moses, a gesture of love and friendship. As the Lord commanded earlier (3:16–17), Aaron and Moses gather the elders, and Aaron, the spokesman, tells them all what the Lord said to Moses, who performs the wondrous signs for them.

Lectio Divina

Spend 8 to 10 minutes in silent contemplation of the following passage:

Aaron will speak to the people whatever Moses directs him to say, and Moses will receive his message from the Lord. When Aaron and Moses go to Pharaoh, God continues to tell them what to say. In the Gospel of Luke, we read that Jesus tells his disciples not to worry about their defense when they drag them before those in authority. He says, "For the holy Spirit will teach you at that moment what you should say" (Luke 12:12).

✠ *What can I learn from this passage?*

Day 3: Pharaoh's Harsh Response (5—6:1)

When Moses and Aaron approach Pharaoh and tell him, "Thus says the LORD, the God of Israel," they are speaking of God whom Pharaoh denies knowing. This could refer to Pharaoh's lack of any knowledge of this God, or that he refuses to acknowledge the God of the Israelites. When Aaron and Moses request that Pharaoh allow them to go on a three-day journey in the wilderness, Pharaoh views their request as a sign of laziness on the part of the Israelite slaves.

Pharaoh orders the Egyptian taskmasters and the Israelite foremen no longer to supply to the Israelite slaves the straw needed for brick making, but to have them gather the straw themselves. The straw mixed with the clay made the bricks more durable when dried in the sun. Pharaoh orders the taskmasters and foremen not to reduce the number of bricks expected of the Israelites. So the taskmasters use the same introduction to the order given that Moses used in speaking of the Lord sending him. The taskmasters say, "Thus says Pharaoh" (5:10), which could be a reference to Pharaoh as a god. Moses began his petition to Pharaoh with the words, "Thus says the Lord" (5:1).

When the Israelites did not reach their allotted number of bricks, the taskmasters beat the foremen. The foremen cry out to Pharaoh just as the Israelites cry out to the Lord. The foremen complain to Aaron and Moses, accusing them of making them oppressed by Pharaoh and his servants and putting a sword into their hands to kill them. Moses becomes discouraged and asks the Lord why God is treating the people so badly and why the Lord sent him. The Lord says that "By a strong hand" (6:1), Pharaoh will let the people go, even to the point of driving them from the land. The "strong hand" appears to refer to God's power.

Lectio Divina

Spend 8 to 10 minutes in silent contemplation of the following passage:

Pharaoh refuses to accept the God of the Hebrews and accuses the Israelites of being lazy because they wish to leave and pray. Those who seek good things in the name of the Lord are often rejected and judged. Jesus was accused of acting in the name of Beelzebul, the prince of demons, but Jesus was able to point out the foolishness of such an accusation. Strange to say, even good deeds can look like they are self-serving to those who reject the one doing them.

✠ *What can I learn from this passage?*

Day 4: Fulfilling God's Promise to the Patriarchs (6:2—7:7)

The following passage comes mostly from the Priestly editor, who mingles together the two traditions, namely the Yahwist tradition and the Eloist tradition (see "Introduction"). There is a parallel to the commissioning of Moses and the role of Aaron found earlier in Exodus (3—4:17), although there are other features added to this passage. For example, in this passage, the Lord is again introduced as the God of Abraham, Isaac, and Jacob, but the author adds that they did not know the name of the Lord, who is here identified as Yahweh. Since the Eloist author did not refer to God as Yahweh, the Priestly author who brings both traditions together has God tell Moses that the Israelites did not identify the Lord as Yahweh until this time.

The Lord pledges to bring the people to the land promised to Abraham, Isaac, and Jacob. The Israelites, however, refuse to listen to Moses' words. When God charges Moses to tell Pharaoh to let the Israelites leave the land, Moses objects, saying that if the Israelites did not listen to him, then how will Pharaoh? The Lord speaks to Moses and Aaron and orders them to bring the Israelites out of Egypt.

The Priestly author places the genealogy here to identify the family line of Aaron and Moses, showing that they belong to the line of Jacob. The genealogy begins with the first two sons of Jacob, Reuben and Simeon, to show that Levi is the third son of Jacob. The line of Levi continues down to Aaron and Moses, who are the ones the Lord sends to speak with Pharaoh. Moses will act as God does, telling Aaron what to say, and Aaron will be like the prophet who speaks in God's name. The Lord will harden the heart of Pharaoh and God will place a heavy judgment on Egypt. Through these acts of the Lord, which will lead to the departure of the Israelites from Egypt, the Egyptians will know that the God of the Israelites is the Lord.

Lectio Divina

Spend 8 to 10 minutes in silent contemplation of the following passage:

Moses actually had good news for the Israelites, but at this point they refuse to listen to him. Jesus had good news for his disciples when he told them that he was the bread of life and that he was going to give them his flesh to eat and his blood to drink. They did not understand that Jesus was speaking of the eucharistic bread and wine that would become the true sacramental presence of his Body and Blood. Many of his disciples left him, but those who remain do not understand, but they trust that they will later understand. Peter asks in the name of those remaining, "Master, to whom shall we go?

You have the words of eternal life" (John 6:68). Trusting God, even in moments of doubt, leads to wisdom.

✠ *What can I learn from this passage?*

Review Questions

1. Why did God have to convince Moses that he was worthy of his call?

2. Why do you think God allowed the Israelites to turn against Moses and Aaron?

3. What is the significance of God speaking to Moses and Moses then speaking to Aaron?

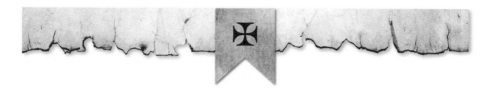

Departure From Egypt

EXODUS 7:8–15

"Remember this day on which you came out of Egypt, out of a house of slavery. For it was with a strong hand that the LORD brought you out from there" (13:3).

Opening Prayer (SEE PAGE 16)

Context

Part 1: Exodus 7:8—8 Aaron and the magicians compete, with God showing Aaron's superiority. The plagues begin. Moses has Aaron stretch out his staff over the waters of Egypt, and all the water in the land turned to blood. When Pharaoh refuses to allow the Israelites to leave, Aaron stretches his hand with the staff over the running water in the land and frogs came up and covered the land. For the third plague, Aaron strikes the dust and the dust turns into gnats that overrun the land. For the fourth plague, flies swarm over the land in every place except for where the Israelites reside.

Part 2: Exodus 9—15 When Pharaoh remains obstinate, the Lord sends the fifth plague, a pestilence that strikes the animals in Egypt, but not the livestock of the Israelites. The sixth plague consists of dust thrown into the air that will cause festering boils. The seventh plague delivers hail that destroys all vegetation except in the land of the Israelites. The eighth plague leads to locusts overrunning the land. The ninth plague brings darkness for three days. The most dreaded plague of all comes with the tenth plague that kills all the firstborn males of humans and animals alike. The first Passover meal is celebrated as the people sacrifice a lamb, share a meal together, and paint the blood of the lamb on their lintels and doorposts. The Lord passes over the homes with the blood on the doorposts and lentils. Pharaoh finally gives permission for the Israelites to depart, but he soon changes his mind and pursues them. The Israelites cross the Reed Sea safely and the Egyptians are inundated as the water returns to the sea.

PART 1: GROUP STUDY (EXODUS 7:8—8)

Read aloud Exodus 7:8—8.

7:8–24 The First Plague

This part of the passage comes from the Priestly author. Since Aaron belongs to the Priestly line of Levi, the Priestly author would naturally favor him. When Pharaoh asks for a sign, Moses is to tell Aaron to throw down his staff. At the moment that Aaron throws down his staff before Pharaoh and his servants, it turns into a serpent. Pharaoh calls in his magicians, who in turn throw down their staffs that also turn into serpents. Aaron's staff, however, swallows their staffs. After witnessing this event, the heart of Pharaoh remains hardened and he would not listen, as foretold by the Lord.

The Lord directs Moses and Aaron to meet Pharaoh on the bank by the Nile where he goes early in the morning. Moses identifies the Lord for Pharaoh as the God of the Hebrews. He receives a message from the Lord to bring his staff with him, but it is Aaron who will perform the miracle with his staff. The passage becomes somewhat confusing here as Moses tells Pharaoh that he will strike the water with his staff and the water of the Nile will turn into blood, the fish will die, and the Nile will stink so that the Egyptians will be unable to drink its water. The threat is not against all the people, but against the Egyptians alone.

After telling Pharaoh that he will strike the water, Moses receives a different message. The confusion comes from the Priestly tradition that is inserted here as the Lord has Moses tell Aaron to stretch out his hand with the staff over the waters of Egypt, and all its streams, canals, ponds, and supplies of water become blood. Aaron strikes the Nile with his staff and all happens as predicted. Pharaoh's magicians do the same with their magic, but this seems unlikely, since all the water in Egypt had already turned to blood. As a result of the action of the magicians, Pharaoh departs with his heart still hardened, leaving the Egyptians to have to dig around the Nile for drinking water.

Some commentators note that the Nile would occasionally turn the color of blood when some small particles of dirt, dust, or organisms would contaminate the water and make it undrinkable. The first nine plagues may be events that did happen occasionally in Egypt, but for the writer, the timing of the event with the action of Aaron or Moses is considered miraculous and meant to be a sign to convince Pharaoh.

7:25—8:15 Frogs and Gnats

After seven days, the Lord again sends Moses to ask Pharaoh to let God's people go. If Pharaoh refuses, the judgment will be a plague of frogs coming into the palace, bedrooms, servants' houses, ovens, kneading bowls, and over all the people. Although it is not mentioned, Pharaoh apparently refused, so the Lord tells Moses to speak to Aaron and have him stretch out his hand with the staff over streams, canals, and ponds to make frogs overrun Egypt. The magicians do the same with their magical arts, but the story seems implausible, since it would seem impossible to decide which frogs came as a result of the power of God or of the magicians. The storytellers were not concerned with such details.

Pharaoh promises to let the Israelites go if Moses and Aaron will remove the frogs from him and the people. Moses wisely seeks a designated time for his prayer so that Pharaoh will know that it is done by the power of the Lord of the Israelites. When Moses cries out to the Lord at the designated time, all the frogs die with the exception of the frogs in the Nile. When Pharaoh sees that the plague had ended, he changes his mind as the Lord foretold.

The Lord directs Moses to tell Aaron to strike the dust with his staff, and the dust will turn into gnats to plague the people and animals alike, which is what happens. The magicians, however, could not use their magic to make this happen, and they inform Pharaoh that the plague is the finger of God at work. Pharaoh's heart remains hardened, despite the words of the magicians.

8:16–28 Flies Cover the Land

Moses now becomes central to the remainder of the plagues and Aaron is rarely mentioned. The Lord tells Moses to meet with Pharaoh early in the morning as he sets out for the water, as he did at the beginning of the first plague. Moses is to reiterate the same request he made before the previous plagues, asking Pharaoh to let the people go or suffer a plague of swarms of flies which will cover Pharaoh, the servants, all the people, the homes, and the ground under their feet. The Lord makes an exception to the plague by saying that it would not touch Goshen, the land of the Hebrews. The plague will not take place immediately, but on the next day it happens.

Pharaoh summons Moses and offers to permit him to sacrifice to his God within the boundaries of Egypt. Moses points out that their sacrifice is abhorrent to the Egyptians. This may have referred to Egyptian sensitivities that identified certain animals with deities. Moses claims that he fears that the Israelites will be stoned if they perform sacrifices that challenge Egyptian beliefs. Pharaoh then promises that they may leave as long as they do not travel too far from Egypt. Moses promises to pray for the end to the plague as soon as he leaves Pharaoh's presence. The plague ends, but Pharaoh again hardens his heart and refuses to allow the Israelites to leave.

Review Questions

1. Which of the first four plagues would you consider the worst?
2. Why did God have Aaron stretch his staff out to bring about some of the plagues?
3. What is the reason that Pharaoh gives for not wanting the Israelites to leave Egypt?

Closing Prayer (SEE PAGE 16)

Pray the closing prayer now or after *lectio divina*.

Lectio Divina (SEE PAGE 9)

Relax your body and maintain a posture of prayer (back straight, eyes shut, feet flat on the floor). This exercise can take as long as you want, but in the context of this Bible study, 10 to 20 minutes should be sufficient.

The meditations that follow are provided only to help group participants use this prayer form, but note that *lectio* is intended to bring one to a place of prayerful contemplation where the Word of God speaks to the hearer from his or her heart. (See page 9 for further instruction.)

The First Plague (7:8–24)

Aaron takes his staff and holds his hands over the waters, and all the water in the land turns to blood. In the Gospel of John, Jesus turns water into wine at a wedding feast in Cana, and the event is connected to his passion. Once he performs the miracle, his journey toward his death and resurrection, which he refers to as his "hour," begins (see John 2:1–11). Jesus will later take the wine at the Last Supper and declare, "This cup is the new covenant of my blood, which will be shed for you" (Luke 22:20). The miracle God performs through Aaron's gesture is far from the miraculous gift of Jesus' blood given to us sacramentally in the Eucharist.

✠ *What can I learn from this passage?*

Frogs and Gnats (7:25—8:15)

The third plague convinces the magicians that the plagues are coming from the hand of God and not through some form of magic. Jesus performed many miracles during his life that convinced some of the people that Jesus was truly the Son of God, but despite his miracles, many refused to believe in him. When Jesus died, the veil of the temple was torn from top to bottom, the earth quaked, rocks split, and bodies rose from the tombs. The Roman soldiers, who scourged and mocked Jesus earlier in the day, proclaim in the midst of this chaos, "Truly, this was the Son of God" (Matthew 27:54). For them, these earthshaking events were not a coincidence or magic. For people of faith, God's guidance and miraculous deeds can still occur as they have through the lives of many saints.

✠ *What can I learn from this passage?*

Flies Cover the Land (8:16–28)

Despite the miracles and plagues that obviously point to a supernatural power, Pharaoh refuses to believe. No matter what God does, Pharaoh will never be able to see the hand of God at work. In the Gospel of Matthew, Jesus does not fast as the Pharisees do, so they view him as a glutton and a drunkard. John the Baptist came as an ascetic, fasting and avoiding drink, so they viewed him as possessed by a demon. Jesus knew that they would reject everything God sends in an effort to convince them of the truth of his message, and he says, "We played a flute for you, but you did not dance, we sang a dirge, but you did not mourn" (Matthew 11:17). Like Pharaoh, they had closed their minds to God's miraculous gifts.

✠ *What can I learn from this passage?*

PART 2: INDIVIDUAL STUDY (EXODUS 9—15)

Day 1: The Fifth to the Tenth Plague (9—11:10)

For the fifth plague, the Lord tells Moses to report to Pharaoh that the Lord will strike the livestock with a very severe pestilence. But the livestock of the Israelites will not suffer the pestilence. All the livestock of the Egyptians die, but not one animal of the Israelites dies. Still, Pharaoh remains obstinate.

For the sixth plague, the Lord speaks to Moses and Aaron and tells them to take a handful of soot from a kiln and, in the presence of Pharaoh, scatter it toward the sky that will turn into fine dust over Egypt. The dust will cause boils on people and animals alike. The magicians are also infested, but the Lord hardens Pharaoh's heart.

Moses again meets Pharaoh early in the morning and warns that the intensity of the next plague will be so severe that they will know that there is none like the God of the Hebrews. God allows the Egyptians to survive to reveal the power of God to all nations. In this plague, the Lord will shower a violent hail upon them. The Lord allows Pharaoh, his servants, and the people to save themselves and their animals by seeking shelter, but not all do. Here, Moses uses his staff for the first time and stretches it toward the sky. Fierce thunder explodes, lightning and hail plummet the earth, annihilating everything in the fields along with all the unsheltered people and animals. In Goshen, no hail fell.

Pharaoh begs Moses and Aaron to pray to the Lord whom Pharaoh now declares to be the just one. He states that he and his people are at fault. Moses promises to pray, knowing that Pharaoh does not yet believe in the Lord God. The author explains that the flax and barley, which already were in the early stages of growth, were destroyed, but the wheat and pelt remained, since they will begin to grow and be destroyed by a later plague. As usual, once all has ended, Pharaoh hardens his heart and refuses to allow the Israelites to leave.

For the next plague, Moses and Aaron warn Pharaoh that Egypt will suffer an overwhelming hoard of locusts that will eat all that was saved in the previous devastation. The locusts will overrun everything: homes, the land, and all the Egyptians. Pharaoh's servants beg Pharaoh to let the Israelites go to serve the Lord, their God. Pharaoh tells Moses and Aaron that they may go, but they must leave their little ones behind. Otherwise, Pharaoh suspects that they would have some evil intent in mind.

As a result of Pharaoh's obstinacy, the Lord tells Moses to stretch out his hand over Egypt so that the plague of the locusts may take place. So many locusts cover the land that it turns black and all vegetation and fruit is destroyed. Pharaoh again repents, asks for forgiveness, and begs that they take this plague from him. Moses prays and a west wind comes and blows the locusts out to the Red Sea. Pharaoh again hardens his heart.

The ninth plague begins with no visit to Pharaoh mentioned. The Lord directs Moses to stretch out his hand toward the sky so that darkness would cover the earth for three days. It was so thick that people could not see each other. Pharaoh summons Moses and Aaron and agrees to let them go, but they must leave their flocks and herds behind. Moses explains that they need all their livestock, since they will not know which ones are to be sacrificed until they get to the place of sacrifice. The Lord hardens Pharaoh's heart, but this time Pharaoh threatens Moses with death if he appears before him again.

In preparation for the tenth plague, the Israelites are to ask their neighbors for silver, gold articles, and clothing. All the Egyptians have apparently turned against Pharaoh and were well disposed toward the Israelites. Moses delivers an oracle from the Lord, saying that about midnight the Lord would go through Egypt and every firstborn of Egypt will die, from the firstborn of Pharaoh, the firstborn of a slave girl, and the firstborn of the animals, causing loud wailing in Egypt. Among the Israelites, not even a dog will grieve, proving that the Lord distinguishes between Egypt and Israel. And finally all the servants of Egypt will come and bow down before the Lord, saying that the Israelites should leave.

Lectio Divina

Spend 8 to 10 minutes in silent contemplation of the following passage:

> Throughout salvation history, God sends prophets such as Moses and Aaron to speak to the people in God's name. Jesus sends out his apostles and disciples to spread his message, and many of them would find their message rejected, just as Moses and Aaron did. In the Gospel of Luke, Jesus sends out the Twelve with the power to perform great deeds and to spread his message about the kingdom of God. Jesus directs them to accept a sign of welcome where it is given, and to shake from their shoes the dust of the places where they are not welcomed (see 9:6). Jesus disciples will always encounter those who accept Jesus' message and those who refuse to listen to Jesus' message.
>
> ✠ *What can I learn from this passage?*

Day 2: The Passover (12)

In the opening lines of this passage, the Priestly author establishes prescriptions for the celebration of the Passover. The feast celebrated actually predates the escape from Egypt, but the Exodus experience gives it a different meaning. It was originally an ancient celebration for nomadic people who shepherded their flock. The shepherds would paint the blood of the lamb on the tent poles to ward off evil spirits and insure the healthy productiveness of the flock.

In the Exodus story, the Lord speaks to Moses and Aaron, establishing the month of the Passover as the first month of the year. On the tenth of the month, all families must take an unblemished, year old lamb or goat from their flock and have it slaughtered at twilight on the fourteenth day of the month. If a family is too small for a lamb, it may join with a neighbor and divide the cost according to the number attending from each household. The blood of the lamb is to be painted on the two doorposts and the lintel of the house where the lamb is eaten. Those celebrating the feast will eat the lamb with unleavened bread and bitter herbs. The lamb must be roasted with its head, shanks, and inner organs. And in the morning, whatever is left over must be burned.

The Lord decrees that the Israelites, prepared for a journey, are to eat the lamb in haste, with their loins girt, sandals on their feet, and a staff in hand. The Lord will pass over the houses with the blood on the doorposts and lintels. The Lord will go through Egypt, killing every firstborn human and animal, proving that the Lord of the Israelites is far more powerful than the gods of the Egyptians.

The Israelites will celebrate the feast of Unleavened Bread around the time of Passover. The Lord declares that the feast is to go from the evening of the fourteenth day of the first month until the evening of the twenty-first day. This passage about the Feast of Unleavened Bread seems to be a later addition, since it speaks as though the Israelites are already in the Promised Land. The passage tells us that the day will commemorate the day the Lord led their Israel armies out of Egypt, as though the event has already taken place. The feast itself, like the feast of the Passover, significantly predates the Exodus event. It came from the Canaanite practice of designating the beginning of the harvest. The Passover had nomadic origins, and the feast of Unleavened Bread had agricultural origins.

The day will be a day of pilgrimage to the Lord. At the time of Jesus' passion, visitors flocked to Jerusalem to celebrate Passover and the feast of Unleavened Bread. On this feast, all leaven must be removed from the house, and for seven days, the people are to eat unleavened bread, no matter where they are. The penalty for those who eat leavened bread during this time is expulsion from Israel. No work is permitted on the first and seventh day, except the necessary work of preparing a meal.

Moses directs the elders to follow the prescriptions established by the Lord. They are to acquire and slaughter a lamb for their families and dip a cluster of hyssop in the blood and paint it on their doorposts and lintels. They are to remain indoors as the Lord passes over their homes and strikes the Egyptians. Moses decrees that they are to commemorate this event when they enter the land promised by the Lord and explain the rite to their children. Hearing these words, the people pay homage to the Lord and do what Moses decreed.

At midnight, the Lord struck dead all the firstborn of the Egyptians, from the highest to the lowest. Some commentators suspect that there was an epidemic of some type that affected the Egyptians, but not the Israelites. As the story came down orally to the scribe who wrote about it, it became embellished to the point that the death of the firstborn took the place of the many who died. Whatever happened, it led to the release of the Israelites from Egypt.

Pharaoh now urges Moses to leave with everyone and everything they have. He seems to recognize the power of the Lord of the Israelites as he tells Moses to go and serve the Lord. The Egyptian people, fearing the Lord of the Israelites, urge them in a panic to leave, lest they all be killed. The Israelites take with them bread before it was leavened and wrap it in their cloaks. As Moses commanded, the Israelites take from the Egyptians articles of silver, gold, and clothing. The Egyptians are eager to allow them to take whatever they wanted, perhaps in an effort to reverence the awesome Lord of the Israelites.

Moses appears to lead the people southeast to a place called Succoth. The author states that the group consisted of 600,000 men, not counting women and children. Counting women and children would make this number inflate well beyond a million people. The number is highly exaggerated, since this large number of people and their animals would not be able to cross the Reed Sea in one night. Many went with them who were from mixed ancestry, which meant that they were not all descendants of Jacob. In their haste, they took only unleavened bread dough that they baked into unleavened bread. Since it was a night of vigil for the Lord, then all Israelites must likewise make it a night of vigil. In their haste when leaving Egypt, the Israelites did not prepare any food for the journey.

The Lord reiterates prescriptions for taking part in the Passover meal. This may be a later addition that was added while the Israelites were in the

Promised Land. No foreigner may eat of the meal unless he is a slave who has been circumcised. No one who is hired or passing through may eat of the lamb. The lamb must not be taken out of the house in which it is eaten, and none of its bones may be broken. Commentators see in this a later reference to Jesus, the Lamb of God, whose bones were not broken as he hung on the cross. It is a community celebration, so the whole community celebrates it at the same time. Anyone considered an alien may take part in the meal if all the males of the family are circumcised.

Lectio Divina

Spend 8 to 10 minutes in silent contemplation of the following passage:

In Matthew's Gospel, we read that Jesus' disciples begin to prepare for the Passover Meal on the first day of the feast of Unleavened Bread. Jesus sends them into the city with the instructions to a certain man, saying that in his house Jesus will be celebrating the Passover with his disciples. At the Passover Meal, Jesus says over the bread, "Take and eat, this is my body," and over the wine, "Drink from it all of you, for this is my blood of the covenant which shall be shed on behalf of the many for the forgiveness of sin." Jesus is the new sacrificial Lamb who introduces a new covenant of his body and blood. For Christians, a new Passover has begun.

✠ *What can I learn from this passage?*

Day 3: Consecration of the Firstborn (13:1–16)

The Lord tells Moses that every firstborn, whether human or animal, belongs to the Lord. The message digresses to a repetition of the prescription of eating unleavened bread. A previous passage concerning the unleavened bread comes from the Priestly author (12:14–20), but the current passage comes from the Yahwist author. Moses calls the people to remember this day and how the Lord led them out of Egypt. He declares that nothing leavened may be eaten during this memorial. Moses also identifies the month with a Canaanite name for the month which is "Abib," named later by the Israelites as "Nisan."

Here, Moses decrees that upon arriving in the Promised Land, they are to celebrate the event in this first month of each year by eating only unleavened bread for seven days. He says that they are to tell their children that the practice comes from the day when the Lord led the Israelites out of Egypt. The celebration will be like a sign on their hand, which may refer to a ring worn on the finger for identification, or a mark on the forehead, which was a ceremonial mark on the foreheads of their neighbors. This passage may have led to the later practice of wearing a small parchment on the forehead which taught about the one God and God's liberation of the Israelites from slavery in Egypt.

The passage returns to the theme of consecrating the firstborn to the Lord. When the people arrive in the land of Canaanites, the land of promise, they are to consecrate every newborn child. Every firstborn animal will belong to the Lord. The firstborn donkey, an unclean animal not worthy of sacrifice, shall be ransomed with a sheep. If the donkey is not ransomed, its neck shall be broken. Every firstborn son shall be ransomed. Moses again tells them to teach their son that this is a reminder of the Lord's liberation of the Israelites from slavery in Egypt when the Lord killed all the firstborn male children and animals of the Egyptians.

Lectio Divina

Spend 8 to 10 minutes in silent contemplation of the following passage:

Mary and Joseph bring the child Jesus to the Temple in response to the Law of Moses that declares that every male child shall be consecrated to the Lord, and the firstborn son shall be ransomed with an offering for sacrifice. Mary and Joseph apparently offer "a pair of turtledoves or two young pigeons" (Luke 2:24), which is an offering ordinarily made by the poor. Mary and Joseph show themselves to be an obedient and pious Jewish couple, intent on fulfilling the demands of the Mosaic Law.

✠ *What can I learn from this passage?*

Day 4: The Red Sea Experience (13:17—15:21)

God did not lead the Hebrews by the shortest route, which was by way of the land of the Philistines, along the shore of the Mediterranean, but God led them toward the Red Sea along the wilderness road. If they traveled the way of the Philistines, the Hebrews would be more likely to encounter Egyptian troops and have to fight them. The Lord feared that the people may turn back rather than fight the Egyptians, so the Lord led them on an indirect route. When Joseph, the son of Jacob, was dying, he made the Israelites pledge that they would take his bones with them when they traveled to the land promised them by God. Moses fulfills the pledge made to Joseph when he takes Joseph's bones with them as they travel to the land where Joseph's ancestors were buried. The Lord led them by means of a cloud during the day and a column of fire at night. This could be the same column of fire that would be surrounded by smoke during the day and visible through the smoke at night.

When Pharaoh learns that the Israelites have left, he again has a change of heart, suddenly aware that he has allowed the slaves who were working on his projects to flee. Pharaoh led an army of all the chariots in Egypt with officers on all of them. They were able to reach the camp of the Hebrews that was by the sea.

When the Israelites realized that the Egyptians were approaching, they became frightened and complained to Moses. Moses tried to allay their fears, telling them that the Lord will fight for them. The episode continues to stress that all is happening for the glory of God. In this event, the Lord directs Moses to stretch out his staff over the sea to split it in two at the appropriate time so that the Israelites may pass through it on dry land. God will receive glory when the Egyptians see the whole army of Pharaoh go after the Israelites. The angel of God present in the cloud moves to the back of the Israelite camp and separates the Egyptian army and the Israelites. At night, the cloud becomes a column of fire that successfully keeps each camp away from the other.

Moses stretches out his hand over the sea and, all night long, the Lord drives back the sea with a strong east wind, turning the sea into dry land. The Israelites enter the sea on dry land, with the water like walls to their right and left. The Egyptians followed after them into the sea, but Moses, following the Lord's command, stretches out his hand over the waters and they begin to flow back upon the Egyptians, destroying them all. When the people saw the dead bodies of the Egyptians on the seashore, they became aware of the great power of God and believed in the Lord and in Moses, the Lord's servant.

The story has a number of Semitic embellishments. If the entire army of Egypt had been destroyed along with Pharaoh, then the enemies of Egypt would easily plunder the nation, which they did not do. The wall of water to the right and left of the Israelites during the crossing presents a stunning picture of God's power, but the mention of the east wind blowing all night gives hints of a natural event which took place periodically in the Reed Sea. The sea is a sea of reeds, not the Red Sea as early false translations named it. When the wind blew, the waters would subside enough for people to walk across. When the wind ceased, the water would flood back in. The wheels of the chariots would naturally become stuck in a swampy area where mud would remain after the water receded.

The author applies an ancient poem to Moses. The poem sings of the gloriously triumphant Lord who has cast horse and chariot into the sea and the Lord as a savior, all images that seem to fit with the destruction of the Egyptians. The poem sings of the power of God over the boastful enemies who were destroyed when the sea covered them. God is praised as being far superior to any god. The astounding works of the Lord are awe-inspiring. The loving God led the Chosen People, guided them, fought for them, and planted them in the sanctuary established by the Lord. Miriam appears in this passage as one who leads the women with tambourines, dancing and singing about the glorious triumph of the Lord.

Lectio Divina

Spend 8 to 10 minutes in silent contemplation of the following passage:

God led the Israelites to the Reed Sea and miraculously opened a path for them through the sea. Leading them in a cloud by day and in a column of fire by night. In John's Gospel, when Jesus is preparing for his death, he promises to send his disciples a helper and guide, the Spirit of truth. Where the people of the Old Testament era had a column of fire and a cloud to guide them, the people of the New Testament will have an Advocate, the Spirit of truth. The Spirit Jesus promises to send will open a path for the Church throughout history. As our guide and helper, the Holy Spirit will open a path through life for each one of us who remains faithful to God.

✠ *What can I learn from this passage?*

Review Questions

1. Which of the plagues from the fifth to the ninth would you consider to be the worst? Explain.

2. What can we learn from the Passover of the Jews? How does this even enrich our Christian understanding of the celebration of Easter?

3. How do you feel about the reality that the Israelites did not actually pass through the Red Sea? Explain your reaction.

LESSON 8

Ten Commandments of the Lord

EXODUS 15:22—40

Now, if you obey me completely and keep my covenant, you will be my treasured possession among all people, though all the earth is mine. You will be to me a kingdom of priests, a holy nation (19:5–6).

Opening Prayer (SEE PAGE ???)

Context

Part 1: Exodus 15:22—17 During their journey through the desert, the people discover a source of water that is too bitter to drink, and they grumble against Moses, but God helps to make the water fresh. The people again grumble for meat and bread, and the Lord responds by giving them quail and manna. When they move on and later become thirsty again, they quarrel with Moses. God directs Moses to strike a specific rock and water flows from the rock. Joshua leads the Israelites in battle against Amalek while Moses prays. As long as Moses' hands are raised up, the Israelites are able to defeat the enemy. Aaron and Hur hold Moses' hands up when he becomes tired.

Part 2: Exodus 18—40 Moses later meets with Jethro, who is identified as his father-in-law. He helps Moses organize the Israelites under judges to arbitrate the people's grievances and requests. The

Israelites arrive at Mount Sinai where God appears to Moses and gives him the Ten Commandments. Moses ratifies a covenant with God at the foot of Mount Sinai by splashing the blood of offered animals on the altar and on the people. Moses goes up the mountain, where he receives the commandments written by God on stone tablets. After forty days, when he comes down the mountain, he finds the people worshiping a golden calf and, in his anger, he throws down the tablets and breaks them. Later, when the Lord in anger wishes to destroy the people, Moses begs the Lord to spare them. Moses asks to see God's face, but is allowed to see only the back of God.

PART 1: GROUP STUDY (EXODUS 15:22—17)

Read aloud Exodus 15:22—17.

15:22—16:36 Life in the Wilderness

In their travels, the Israelites arrive at a place known as Marah, which means "bitter." When they find that the water there is bitter, the people grumble against Moses, who pleads with the Lord, asking what they are to drink. At the Lord's bidding, Moses casts a piece of wood into the water, and the water becomes fresh. This was a place where God put them to a test.

A month after they leave Egypt, the Israelites come into the wilderness of Sin, which is between Elim and Sinai. The people look back to their days in Egypt and, forgetting the misery they endured, they wish they had died in Egypt where they at least had meat in their kettles and bread. Moses reminds the Israelites that in grumbling against him and Aaron, they are really grumbling against the Lord. The Lord directs Moses to tell the people that the Lord has heard their grumbling and will send them meat at twilight and bread in the morning. God, however, puts them to the test by directing them to gather their daily portion each day and on the sixth day to gather a double portion.

In the evening quail covered the camp. It was not unusual for quail to come to the Sinai area. The migrating quail had flown a long distance when they stop to rest at Sinai. Their exhaustion makes them fairly easy to capture. In the morning, when the dew evaporated, the Israelites find fine flakes of hoarfrost on the ground. Moses had to inform them that it was the bread the Lord is giving them to eat. It was manna, a substance formed by insects that infests the leaves in the area. The substance falls from the leaves and becomes firm during the night. It must be gathered before the morning heat melts it.

The regulations regarding the manna are repeated. Some gather more than they need and some are unable to gather enough. Those who gathered more discover that they did not have the expected abundance, and those who gathered less found that they had enough. Despite Moses' warning not to save any until the morning, some do so and find it wormy and reeking. On the sixth day, they gather enough for two days and find that on the seventh day, the leftovers were not wormy and reeking. Moses declares that the seventh day is a day of rest, the sabbath of the Lord. On the seventh day, some go out to gather more manna, but they find none.

Moses directs Aaron to take a jar, which is a golden vessel, and to put manna in it and then to place it before the Lord for future generations. Aaron places it in front of the Ark of the Covenant. This passage comes from a later time when the people had the Ark.

17 Water From the Rock

The Israelites quarrel with Moses, demanding that he give them water to drink. Moses asks why they quarrel with him and put the Lord to the test. The people again forget how difficult their lives were in Egypt and ask why Moses brought them up out of Egypt to have them die of thirst with their children and livestock. The Lord directs Moses to take some of the elders, go before the people, strike the rock in Horeb, and the water will flow from it. The place received the name Massah, which means "the place of the test," and Meribah, which means "the place of quarreling," because the people tested the Lord there.

Before the Israelites appeared in the area, the Amalekites were a nomadic group that laid claim to southern Palestine and the Sinai peninsula. When Amalek comes to engage the Israelites in battle, Moses sends Joshua and some of the men to fight him. This is the first mention of Joshua, who appears here with no further introduction. Moses tells Joshua that he will be standing at the top of the hill with the staff of God in his hand. As long as Moses keeps his hands raised up, Israel was winning the battle with Amalek, but when Moses lets his hands rest, Amalek began to win. Aaron and Hur have Moses sit on a rock, and they support his hands, one on each side. Joshua defeats Amalek. As a result of the victory, Moses builds an altar and names the place Yahweh-nissi, which means "the Lord is my banner."

Review Questions

1. What does God's response to the grumbling of the Israelites tell us about the image of God found in these chapters?

2. Can you make a comparison in our world today with the people longing for the fleshpots of Egypt? Explain.

Closing Prayer (SEE PAGE 16)

Pray the closing prayer now or after *lectio divina*.

Lectio Divina (SEE PAGE 9)

Relax your body and maintain a posture of prayer (back straight, eyes shut, feet flat on the floor). This exercise can take as long as you want, but in the context of this Bible study, 10 to 20 minutes should be sufficient.

The meditations that follow are provided only to help group participants use this prayer form, but note that *lectio* is intended to bring one to a place of prayerful contemplation where the Word of God speaks to the hearer from his or her heart. (See page 9 for further instruction.)

Life in the Wilderness (15:22—16:36)

Shortly after the journey begins, the Israelites are accusing Moses of endangering their lives with a lack of food and drink. In Matthew's Gospel, Jesus faces a similar type of temptation. Jesus has fasted forty days and forty nights and he was hungry. The tempter comes to Jesus and proposes that since he is the Son of God, he should command the stones of the desert to become bread. Where the Israelites allowed their hunger to tempt them to cry out against God, Jesus refuses to thwart God's plan by changing stones into bread just to alleviate his own hunger. Unlike the Israelites, Jesus overcomes the temptation and shows his trust in God when he says, "One does not live by bread alone, but by every word that comes forth from the mouth of God" (Matthew 4:4). Where the Israelites failed, Jesus succeeded.

✠ *What can I learn from this passage?*

Water from the Rock (17)

Because of the stubbornness of the Israelites, God becomes angry with them. Their quarrelling becomes the source for Psalm 95, later warning the Israelites: "Do not harden your hearts as at Meribah, as on the day of Massah in the desert. There your ancestors tested me; they tried me though they had seen my works. Forty years I loathed that generation; I said: 'This people's heart goes astray; they do not know my ways.' Therefore I swore in my anger: 'They shall not enter into my rest'" (95:8–11).

✠ *What can I learn from this passage?*

PART 2: INDIVIDUAL STUDY (EXODUS 18—40)

Day 1: Moses and Jethro Organize the People (18)

Jethro comes to Moses with Moses' wife Zipporah and their two sons. The two sons have names that express Moses' situation at the time of their birth. The one son, Gershom, who was born when Moses lived in exile from Egypt, means "I am a resident in a foreign land." The second son, Eliezer, meaning "The God of my father is my help; he has rescued me from Pharaoh's sword," was apparently born when Moses was experiencing God's help in Egypt. Moses informs Jethro of all he has endured and how the Lord rescued them. Jethro, who is a Midian priest, professes his belief that the Lord is greater than all the gods. Jethro brings a burnt offering and sacrifices for God. A burnt offering is an offering that is offered and completely burned. Aaron and the elders share a meal before God with Jethro, meaning that they accept Jethro as one in faith with them.

Jethro notices that Moses is judging the people from morning until night. Jethro advises Moses to act as the people's representative before God and bring their disputes to God in order to teach them concerning statutes and instructions. He should then choose trustworthy men and set them over the people, breaking the groups down into manageable groups, and have them make all routine decisions. They can refer all important cases to Moses. So Moses does as Jethro suggests.

Lectio Divina

Spend 8 to 10 minutes in silent contemplation of the following passage:

We could easily overlook the need for Moses to organize the large group of people he is leading into segments so that grievances may be judged and concerns may be voiced. In the Gospel of Luke, Jesus feeds 5,000 men and most likely many more women and children. To make the situation manageable, Jesus tells his disciples to have them sit in groups of about fifty. Good organization allows for better ministry. Administration is a ministry in the Church.

✠ *What can I learn from this passage?*

Day 2: The Great Theophany at Sinai (19)

The people come to the wilderness of Sinai and encamp at the foot of the mountain, which bears the name Horeb or Sinai. This is Moses' second visit to the mountain, since it was on this mountain that God spoke to him from a burning bush. Moses ascends the mountain to meet the Lord. The Lord tells Moses that if the Israelites will obey the Lord completely and keep the covenant, they will be the Lord's treasured possession on earth. They will be a kingdom of priests, God's holy nation. As a result of such a gift, the Israelites will have to follow certain purification rites. However, this gift of priesthood differs from that given to Christians in their baptism by Christ.

God does not force the Israelites to accept this special gift and the obligations involved. When the elders and the people agree to do all that the Lord asks, Moses brings their response to the Lord. Moses is now clearly God's mediator with the people and the people's mediator with God.

The Lord tells Moses to prepare the people by having them sanctify themselves, wash their garments, and be ready on the third day when the Lord will come down on Mount Sinai in the sight of all the people. The mountain becomes a sacred place, the place of God's visitation. The people are not to go up the mountain or even touch the edge of it. All those who touch it must be put to death, and no one may touch those who are to be killed. Death must come through stoning or being killed with arrows. Only when the people receive a signal from the sound of the ram's horn may they go up the mountain. During the time of preparation, all sexual intercourse is prohibited.

The visitation from God comes in true Semitic fashion, with great thunder, lightning, and clouds. Added to the Lord's visitation is a loud blast from the shofar, the ram's horn that sounds like a trumpet. The author makes no mention of any individual blowing the horn. Moses leads the people out to the foot of Mount Sinai, which is completely covered with smoke, since the Lord is coming down upon it in fire. In true Semitic fashion, the mountain trembles at the awe-inspiring presence of God.

The Lord directs Moses to tell the people, under penalty of death, not to break through the cloud to see the Lord. The priests must sanctify themselves to avoid God's anger. Moses explains that this command may not be necessary, since there are already boundaries around the mountain that make it sacred. The Lord tells Moses to go down and bring up Aaron with him, but the warning about the priests and people not breaking through still stands.

Lectio Divina

Spend 8 to 10 minutes in silent contemplation of the following passage:

In the Scriptures, a mountain is often the place of God's visitation to people. On Mount Sinai, God speaks to Moses and allows him to experience the glory of God. In the Gospel of Matthew, Jesus chooses Peter, James, and John to witness his transfiguration when his countenance shines like the sun (see Matthew 17:1–8). These events did not take place for the chosen witnesses alone, but for all people who read the Scriptures and learn of God's love and concern for creation through them. Moses was the mediator, but the visitation was for the Chosen People of Israel. We honor those who bring God's message to us, but we must remember that the message is given to all of us who must make it part of our lives.

✠ *What can I learn from this passage?*

Day 3: The Ten Commandments (20:11–26)

The Ten Commandments suddenly interrupt the flow of the story with no introduction. Sudden changes such as this show that the final Priestly editor of the Book of Exodus often mingles the various traditions together. The first three commandments have more lengthy explanations than the remaining seven. Commentators believe that later traditions have expanded the original opening commandments which refer to God.

The First Commandment identifies the Lord as the one who led the people out of slavery in Egypt. This call for the Israelites to worship the one true God differs from the practice of other religious people of their day who worshiped more than one god. Many of those led out of slavery in Egypt were people of their own era who believed in many gods. The expression "no gods besides me" could mean for some that there are other gods, but the Lord of the Israelites is the sole God to be worshiped. The idea of only one God is contained in this command. There were many images made of false gods, but the God of the Israelites forbade the making of any image of the true God. God is a jealous God who demands worship alone and who inflicts those who disobey.

The Second Commandment forbids taking the name of the Lord, God, in vain. This originally referred to using the Lord's name in an evil manner, such as swearing falsely. Eventually it referred to the use of the name "Yahweh," which to many became so sacred that the people would use "Adonai," which means "Lord," instead of using the most sacred name of Yahweh for God.

The Third Commandment demands keeping the Sabbath holy. Keeping the Sabbath holy was practiced before the Ten Commandments were given. The reason for keeping the Sabbath holy is to follow the Lord's example as shown in the creation of the world. For the Lord blessed the Sabbath and made it holy.

The Fourth Commandment commands honoring one's father and mother. This was an extremely strict commandment to the people of ancient times. Even before God chose the family of Abraham, we read about Ham, the son of Noah, who is cursed because he ridiculed his father when he became drunk and lay naked inside his tent (Genesis 9:20–27).

The remaining commandments are concise statements that need little explaining. Any one of these sins could be disruptive to the members of a community who depend on each other, as the Israelites do. The Fifth Commandment forbids killing another and has as its foundation the sacredness of life. Killing in battle is not included here, but it refers to killing in the sense of murdering. In its earliest setting, the prohibition to kill referred to the sin of one Israelite killing another Israelite. The Sixth Commandment protects the sanctity of marriage and forbids adultery. The Seventh Commandment forbids stealing, which protects another's property, including all material goods. The Eighth Commandment forbids swearing falsely or bearing false witness against one's neighbor. The Ninth and Tenth Commandments forbid intending to take the wife or goods of another if an opportunity allows.

The passage in 19:25 continues where the last chapter ended. The thunder, the lightning, the blast from the ram's horn, and the smoking mountain frighten the people so much that they back away from the mountain and in fear beg Moses to speak to them rather than allow God to speak to them. They fear that if God speaks to them, they will die. The frightened people stand back as Moses approaches the dark cloud where God is present.

The Lord directs Moses to remind the people that they have now heard the voice of God from heaven. God now orders them not to make gods of silver or gold, as was the custom among those who believed in many gods. The altar to the Lord should be simple and pure, built up from dirt or made from stone which has not been profaned by a chisel. They are to offer burnt offerings, or communion sacrifices of sheep and oxen, which are shared by the people in communion with God. An ironic line adds that the altar should not be raised, apparently to address the idea that a raised altar would expose the privates of the one making the offering.

Lectio Divina

Spend 8 to 10 minutes in silent contemplation of the following passage:

God gave the commandments to the Israelites to help them know what is sinful and harmful to the community. Jesus built on the commandments when he went up a mountain and told his followers how they should think and act as his followers. Blessed are the poor in spirit, for theirs is the kingdom of heaven. These are those who realize that all they have comes from God and belongs to God (see Matthew 5:1). Each one of the Beatitudes involves living all the commandments. Jesus sums up God's law by saying, "Do unto others whatever you would have them do to you. This is the law and the prophets" (Matthew 7:12). The commandments given to Moses concern our relationship to God and all others who share this world with us.

✠ *What can I learn from this passage?*

Laws (21—23)

(Read the note about laws in the "Introduction: Pentateuch I," page 19.)

In these chapters, Moses supposedly receives a series of specific laws from the Lord, but many of the laws obviously concern matters that arose after the Israelites settled in the Promised Land. The reader may choose to scan or skip these chapters and return to the narrative section in chapter 24.

These laws concern the rights of owners over slaves and some rights of slaves when they are mistreated. They establish norms for treating those who afflict personal injury on a person. In this section, we read about equal justice, where a person takes a "life for life, eye for eye, tooth for tooth, hand for hand, foot for foot, burn for burn, wound for wound, stripe for stripe" (21:23–25). By this law, a person could not seek more than the crime that was inflicted. For example, a person may not kill another who has inflicted some injury, but has not taken a life. Furthermore, in this section you will read bout property laws, laws concerning loans of any kind, laws concerning justice within the community, religious laws, and rewards from God for remaining faithful to God's commands.

Day 4: Ratification of the Covenant (24)

The Lord tells Moses to come up the mountain with Aaron and his sons Nadab and Abibu and seventy elders of Israel. But only Moses may come close to the Lord, and the others with him are not to come close, but are to bow down at a distance.

The first three verses, which come from the Yahwist tradition, place Moses on the mountain, but the next verses, from the Eloist tradition, picture Moses coming down to the people. The people agree to all the Lord asks of them. Moses writes down the words of the Lord and, rising early the next morning, he builds an altar of twelve sacred stones for the twelve tribes of Israel. Moses is the only one permitted to write the words of the Lord and build the altar. He takes the blood from the communion offering and puts half of it in bowls and the rest he splashes on the altar. The altar represents the Lord.

Moses reads from the book of the covenant and the people acclaim their willingness to do all that the Lord asks. He then splashes blood on the people, alluding to it as the blood of the covenant that the Lord made with the people. In these actions, Moses has ratified the covenant between God and the Israelites.

In the Yahwist tradition that follows, Moses goes up with Aaron, Nadab, Abihu, and seventy elders of Israel, and they all behold the God of Israel. They ate and drank, which is the Yahwist's idea of ratifying the covenant with a sacrificial meal.

God calls Moses up the mountain to have him receive the commandments written on stone tablets. Moses goes up with Joshua, who is now identified as Moses' assistant. He leaves the elders with Aaron and Hur, who will settle any complaints they may have. For six days, a cloud covers the mountain as the glory of the Lord settles upon it. After the cloud covers the mountain for six days, the Lord calls Moses on the seventh day. Moses enters the cloud, where he remains for forty days and forty nights.

Lectio Divina

Spend 8 to 10 minutes in silent contemplation of the following passage:

The number forty appears often in the Scriptures, and it often means a time of testing or struggle. Moses enters the cloud and remains there for forty days and forty nights, symbolizing his unity with the Lord. Later in the gospels, we will read that Jesus spent forty days and forty nights in the wilderness among the wild animals, which could be a reference to evil spirits. The Israelites will spend forty years in the desert on their journey to the Promised Land. After this, forty for some came to designate a lifetime. Symbolically, forty days and forty nights could refer to a lifetime with the Lord.

✠ *What can I learn from this passage?*

Liturgical Plans (25—31)

These chapters concern the construction of implements used for worship, including the Ark of the Covenant. They also speak of vestments and a rite for consecration of priests, an altar of incense, and the incense itself. Specifying who is to work on these liturgical items, the passages end with regulations for the Sabbath.

The reader may scan or skip these passages and move on to the narrative section in chapter 32.

Day 5: The Golden Calf (32—33:6)

With Moses missing for such a long period of time, the people become restless and ask Aaron to make gods who will go before them. The people are returning to some of the pagan practices they learned in Egypt. Aaron gathers whatever gold the people have and he fashions the gold into a molten calf. Although the people cry out that these are the gods of Israel, Aaron builds an altar and declares that the next day is a feast of the Lord. What he has done by making a golden calf is to make a false image of the one God. The next day, the people offer their burnt offering and communion offering and, after sitting down to eat and drink, they rise to celebrate.

On the mountain, the Lord reveals to Moses that the people are acting sinfully. The Lord tells Moses about the golden calf and the cry of the people in worship saying that these are Israel's gods. The Lord declares that the Israelites are a "stiff-necked" (32:9) people. The Lord is ready to destroy these people and raise up a great nation from Moses. There seems to be an implication that Moses will become a descendant upon whom the promise to the patriarchs falls. The Messiah will come from the line of Judah, not from the line of Levi to which Moses belongs.

Moses urges the Lord to reconsider destroying the Israelites, since they are the Lord's own people, the ones whom the Lord brought out of Egypt with a powerful hand. This would give the Egyptians an opportunity to mock the Lord as acting with an evil intent, killing the Israelites on the mountain and wiping them off the face of the earth. Moses begs the Lord to remember Abraham, Isaac, and Israel and how the Lord swore that their offspring would be as numerous as the stars. The Lord also gave them the promise of the land. As a result of Moses' prayer intention, the Lord relented.

Moses comes down the mountain carrying the two stone tablets written on both sides by God and containing the commandments. Joshua, who was with Moses, hears the noise from the camp and states that there was a battle taking place in the camp. Moses says that it is neither the sound of victory, nor that of defeat, but it is singing. Despite the words of the Lord on the mountain concerning what was happening in the camp, Moses seems unaware of what is taking place. This may be because the editor drew upon two different traditions for this episode. When Moses sees the calf and the dancing, he casts down the stones in anger and they break. He burns the calf, grinds it to dust, pours the dust over the drinking water, and makes the Israelites drink it.

When Moses asks Aaron how he could do such a thing, Aaron blames the people as being prone to evil, saying that they begged him to make a god to go before them. Aaron exonerates himself by saying that he collected the gold, put it in the fire, and the golden calf came out of it, as though Aaron himself had nothing to do with constructing the calf. Moses sees how Aaron has lost control of the crowd, and he cries out for those who are faithful to the Lord to come to him. All the Levites come, and he tells them he is speaking the words of the Lord. They are to go through the camp and kill brothers, friends, and neighbors. They killed about three thousand people that day. Moses installs the Levites as priests that day, because they were willing to go against their own sons and brothers to receive a blessing from the Lord.

The next day, Moses tells the people he will approach the Lord for them, seeking atonement for the grave sin they have committed. Moses asks the Lord to forgive the people, and if the Lord did not wish to do so, then Moses asks the Lord to blot him out of the book the Lord has written. This comes from an image of the Lord having a book with the names of all the living in it. Moses is asking the Lord to take his life. The Lord states that only the one who sinned will be blotted out of the Lord's book. Now, Moses is to lead the people where God directed, promising that an angel will go before them. The Lord sends a veiled message by adding that when it is time to punish, the Lord will punish the people for their sin.

The Lord directs Moses to lead the people toward the land promised to Abraham, Isaac, and Jacob, the land that will be given to their descendants. The Lord will help them drive out the inhabitants of the land, but the Lord will not go with them, since they are a stiff-necked people. The implication seems to be that God may finally become so angry with their stubbornness and grumbling that the Lord may cause some disaster on the way. The people realize their need for the Lord's protection, and as a symbol of their repentance, they no longer wear any ornaments. It was through the use of ornaments that the golden calf was able to be made. Keeping in mind that the Lord relented because of Moses' appeals for the people, the author seems to imply that God still remains angry with the Israelites. God does not ask only that the Israelites not wear their ornaments, but God wants them to rid themselves of their ornaments completely—they must strip them off.

Lectio Divina

Spend 8 to 10 minutes in silent contemplation of the following passage:

The significance of the golden calf is not hard for us to understand, since we live in a society where gold or wealth of any kind has become a golden calf or idol that many people worship. Jesus knows human nature's desire to possess wealth, and he warns us not to store up treasures here on earth that can be destroyed, but to store up treasures in heaven that will last eternally. He tells us that we cannot serve two masters, that is, we "cannot serve God and mammon" (Matthew 6:24).

✠ *What can I learn from this passage?*

Day 6: Moses' Intimacy With God (33:7—34)

At a distance outside the camp, Moses pitches a tent where those who want to consult the Lord may go. Joshua, Moses' assistant, never leaves the tent. When Moses goes to the tent, the people know that the Lord will come down in a column of cloud at the entrance of the tent and speak with Moses. When this happens, the people would bow down at the entrance of their own tents, a gesture that expresses their belief that God was at the entrance of the tent. At the entrance, the Lord speaks to Moses face to face, as a friend speaks to a friend.

Moses' conversation with the Lord returns to the previous passage in which God refused to travel with the Israelites. Moses asks to know the Lord's way, since the Lord has already expressed that Moses is his favored one. The leader of the Israelites needs to know if the Lord will be traveling with them. Because the Lord views Moses as an intimate friend, the Lord promises to go with the Israelites.

Moses becomes bolder, asking to see the Lord's face. Two traditions seem to be mixed together here, since the passage began by saying that the Lord and Moses spoke face to face. The Lord will indeed reward Moses by making the entire Lord's goodness pass before Moses, and the Lord will allow Moses to know the intimate name of God, but Moses may not look at the Lord's face, since the one who looks upon the face of the Lord will die. These words seem to be contradicted, since there are other stories in the Book of Genesis where Hagar claims to have seen the face of God (16:13), and Jacob also makes the same claim (32:31). They both live after seeing the Lord. The Lord tells Moses where to stand, and when the Lord passes by, the Lord will cover Moses' face with the Lord's hand. After the Lord passes, the hand of the Lord will be removed, and Moses will see the Lord's back.

The Lord directs Moses to come up the mountain the next day with two stone tablets like the ones that were broken, intending to write the commandments on them. On his previous trip up the mountain, Moses took Joshua with him, but this time he takes no one. The Lord comes to Moses and shares with him the intimate name of Yahweh, the Lord who is gracious and merciful, slow to anger, and abounding in love and fidelity, whose love goes on for a thousand generations, forgiving yet punishing the children to the third and fourth generation because of the parents' wickedness. Some other scriptural texts which make use of this passage make no mention about punishment from one generation to the next (see Deuteronomy 7:9–10). Moses again asks the Lord to come along with them. Moses admits that they are a stubborn people, but he seeks pardon for their wickedness and sins and claims that they are the Lord's own.

The Lord responds by making a covenant. The Lord will drive out the people inhabiting the land promised to Moses' ancestors. They are to tear down the pagan altars, smash their sacred stones, and cut down their asherahs. The asherahs were wooden poles honoring Asherah, a Canaanite goddess. The God of Israel is a jealous God who will not tolerate any other gods. They must not turn toward these gods nor marry the daughters of those who worship them, lest they themselves become idolaters.

God continues to explain how to practice God's law. They shall not make for themselves molten gods. They are to keep the festival of Unleavened Bread and recognize that all males, animal and human alike, belong to the Lord. They may work six days, but keep the Sabbath for rest, even during the plowing and harvesting time.

They shall keep the feast of Weeks, which is a feast that symbolizes gratitude to God for the harvest. The Israelites celebrate the feast seven weeks or fifty days after the beginning of the harvest. The feast coincides with Pentecost which was originally a Jewish feast commemorating the time when God gave Moses the Law on Sinai. The author repeats the laws involving sacrifice.

Acting on the Lord's command, Moses writes down the words of the Law and remains with the Lord for forty days and forty nights without eating or drinking. When Moses comes down the mountain with the two tablets of the covenant, his face is radiant. Aaron and the other Israelites are afraid to come near him. Moses speaks to them, and thereafter, when he speaks to the people, he puts a veil over his face and removes the veil only when he enters the presence of the Lord. After speaking with the Lord, he tells the Israelites all that he had been commanded.

Lectio Divina

Spend 8 to 10 minutes in silent contemplation of the following passage:

The passage is confusing because of the mingling of various traditions, but the human image of God as found in the Yahwist tradition dominates much of the narrative. Moses and God are friends. Jesus referred to his disciples as friends when he told them that he no longer calls them slaves (in the sense of servants), but friends. He tells them that no one has a greater love than the one who lays down one's life for a friend. Through Jesus' life and death, we are intimate friends of Jesus.

✠ *What can I learn from this passage?*

Special Directives for Worship (35—40)

These chapters repeat much of the religious directives found in chapters 25 to 31. The reader may wish to scan this section or skip over it.

In 40:34–38, the Priestly author speaks of a cloud covering the tent of meeting, which designates the glory of the Lord filling the tabernacle. When the cloud over the tent lifts, the people would move forward, but when it does not lift, the people do not move forward.

Review Questions

1. What is significant about the great Theophany Moses experiences on Mount Sinai?
2. How do each of the Ten Commandments help the people wandering in the desert?
3. What are some examples of people worshiping a golden calf or idol today? Explain.